"Congress shall make
no law … abridging
the freedom of speech,
or of the press."

*First Amendment to the US Constitution*

The basic foundation of our democracy is the First Amendment
guarantee of freedom of expression. The Opposing Viewpoints
series is dedicated to the concept of this basic freedom and the
idea that it is more important to practice it than to enshrine it.

OPPOSING
VIEWPOINTS®
SERIES

# The #MeToo Movement

# Other Books of Related Interest

## Opposing Viewpoints Series

Black Lives Matter
Feminism
Identity Politics
Toxic Masculinity

## At Issue Series

Campus Sexual Violence
Gender Politics
Male Privilege
Sexual Consent

## Current Controversies Series

Freedom of Speech on Campus
Microaggressions, Safe Spaces, and Trigger Warnings
Political Correctness
Whistleblowers

# OPPOSING VIEWPOINTS® SERIES

# The #MeToo Movement

M. M. Eboch, Book Editor

GREENHAVEN PUBLISHING

# 1107804774

Published in 2020 by Greenhaven Publishing, LLC
353 3rd Avenue, Suite 255, New York, NY 10010

Articles in Greenhaven Publishing anthologies are often edited for length to meet page
requirements. In addition, original titles of these works are changed to clearly present
the main thesis and to explicitly indicate the author's opinion. Every effort is made to
ensure that Greenhaven Publishing accurately reflects the original intent of the authors.
Every effort has been made to trace the owners of the copyrighted material.

Cover image: Sarah Morris/Getty Images

**Library of Congress Cataloging-in-Publication Data**

Names: Eboch, M. M., editor.
Title: The #MeToo movement / M.M. Eboch, book editor.
Description: First edition. | New York : Greenhaven Publishing, 2020. | Series: Opposing
viewpoints | Includes bibliographical references and index. | Audience: Grades 9-12.
Identifiers: LCCN 2019022865 | ISBN 9781534505971 (library
binding) | ISBN 9781534505964 (paperback)
Subjects: LCSH: Sexual abuse victims—Juvenile literature. | Sex crimes—
Prevention—Juvenile literature. | Sexual harassment of women—Prevention—
Juvenile literature. | Social movements—Juvenile literature.
Classification: LCC HV6556 .M48 2020 | DDC 362.883—dc23
LC record available at https://lccn.loc.gov/2019022865

*Manufactured in the United States of America*

Website: http://greenhavenpublishing.com

# Contents

## Chapter 1: Is the #MeToo Movement Good for Society?

## Chapter 2: Has #MeToo Gone Too Far?

## Chapter 3: Whom Should We Believe?

## Chapter 4: How Will the #MeToo Movement Change the Future?

# The Importance of Opposing Viewpoints

Perhaps every generation experiences a period in time in which the populace seems especially polarized, starkly divided on the important issues of the day and gravitating toward the far ends of the political spectrum and away from a consensus-facilitating middle ground. The world that today's students are growing up in and that they will soon enter into as active and engaged citizens is deeply fragmented in just this way. Issues relating to terrorism, immigration, women's rights, minority rights, race relations, health care, taxation, wealth and poverty, the environment, policing, military intervention, the proper role of government—in some ways, perennial issues that are freshly and uniquely urgent and vital with each new generation—are currently roiling the world.

If we are to foster a knowledgeable, responsible, active, and engaged citizenry among today's youth, we must provide them with the intellectual, interpretive, and critical-thinking tools and experience necessary to make sense of the world around them and of the all-important debates and arguments that inform it. After all, the outcome of these debates will in large measure determine the future course, prospects, and outcomes of the world and its peoples, particularly its youth. If they are to become successful members of society and productive and informed citizens, students need to learn how to evaluate the strengths and weaknesses of someone else's arguments, how to sift fact from opinion and fallacy, and how to test the relative merits and validity of their own opinions against the known facts and the best possible available information. The landmark series Opposing Viewpoints has been providing students with just such critical-thinking skills and exposure to the debates surrounding society's most urgent contemporary issues for many years, and it continues to serve this essential role with undiminished commitment, care, and rigor.

The key to the series's success in achieving its goal of sharpening students' critical-thinking and analytic skills resides in its title—

Opposing Viewpoints. In every intriguing, compelling, and engaging volume of this series, readers are presented with the widest possible spectrum of distinct viewpoints, expert opinions, and informed argumentation and commentary, supplied by some of today's leading academics, thinkers, analysts, politicians, policy makers, economists, activists, change agents, and advocates. Every opinion and argument anthologized here is presented objectively and accorded respect. There is no editorializing in any introductory text or in the arrangement and order of the pieces. No piece is included as a "straw man," an easy ideological target for cheap point-scoring. As wide and inclusive a range of viewpoints as possible is offered, with no privileging of one particular political ideology or cultural perspective over another. It is left to each individual reader to evaluate the relative merits of each argument— as he or she sees it, and with the use of ever-growing critical-thinking skills—and grapple with his or her own assumptions, beliefs, and perspectives to determine how convincing or successful any given argument is and how the reader's own stance on the issue may be modified or altered in response to it.

This process is facilitated and supported by volume, chapter, and selection introductions that provide readers with the essential context they need to begin engaging with the spotlighted issues, with the debates surrounding them, and with their own perhaps shifting or nascent opinions on them. In addition, guided reading and discussion questions encourage readers to determine the authors' point of view and purpose, interrogate and analyze the various arguments and their rhetoric and structure, evaluate the arguments' strengths and weaknesses, test their claims against available facts and evidence, judge the validity of the reasoning, and bring into clearer, sharper focus the reader's own beliefs and conclusions and how they may differ from or align with those in the collection or those of their classmates.

Research has shown that reading comprehension skills improve dramatically when students are provided with compelling, intriguing, and relevant "discussable" texts. The subject matter of these collections could not be more compelling, intriguing, or urgently relevant to today's students and the world they are poised to inherit. The anthologized articles and the reading and discussion questions that are included with them also provide the basis for stimulating, lively, and passionate classroom debates. Students who are compelled to anticipate objections to their own argument and identify the flaws in those of an opponent read more carefully, think more critically, and steep themselves in relevant context, facts, and information more thoroughly. In short, using discussable text of the kind provided by every single volume in the Opposing Viewpoints series encourages close reading, facilitates reading comprehension, fosters research, strengthens critical thinking, and greatly enlivens and energizes classroom discussion and participation. The entire learning process is deepened, extended, and strengthened.

For all of these reasons, Opposing Viewpoints continues to be exactly the right resource at exactly the right time—when we most need to provide readers with the critical-thinking tools and skills that will not only serve them well in school but also in their careers and their daily lives as decision-making family members, community members, and citizens. This series encourages respectful engagement with and analysis of opposing viewpoints and fosters a resulting increase in the strength and rigor of one's own opinions and stances. As such, it helps make readers "future ready," and that readiness will pay rich dividends for the readers themselves, for the citizenry, for our society, and for the world at large.

# Introduction

> *"I don't really care why men aren't attacking women or aren't firing women off their movie sets, I don't care if they need a mercenary motive for it—I care that society empowers and punishes the right thing."*
>
> —Deborah Frances-White, aka The Guilty Feminist,
> *"Has #MeToo Gone Too Far? The Guilty Feminist Has Her Say,"* by Sinann Fetherston, Raidió Teilifís Éireann,
> January 30, 2018.

The phrase "Me Too" exploded into the public consciousness in 2017. But the term, or what it stood for, was hardly new. For thousands of years, women and girls—and some men and boys—have been the victims of sexual violence. They face sexual harassment from bosses, coworkers, professors, classmates, and even friends. In 2006, Tarana Burke coined the phrase "Me Too." Burke had been working with survivors of sexual violence, especially young women of color from low-wealth communities. She wanted to help survivors find a path to healing. She invited workshop victims to state "Me Too" if they needed help.

On October 15, 2017, MeToo went viral. Actress Alyssa Milano re-tweeted a MeToo tweet. She added, "If you've been sexually harassed or assaulted write 'me too' as a reply to this tweet." The movement quickly went viral with the hashtag #MeToo. As news stories covered the explosive movement, Burke and her work gained publicity.

Today the #MeToo movement tries to help women of every race, from every class, working in every field. It embraces men who have suffered sexual harassment and violence, as well as trans men and women. Tens of thousands of people have announced, "Me

Too." This helps take away the stigma surrounding assault, which too often blames the victim. The movement also helps survivors find community support and resources for healing. The ultimate goal is to put an end to sexual violence.

It's hard to imagine anyone openly criticizing a movement intended to stop violence and harassment. And yet, many people have criticized.

The #MeToo movement allowed women to publicly accuse men of crimes and other bad behavior. Their claims could quickly gain attention on social media and in the news. A few men faced criminal charges and were convicted by the law. Several powerful men lost their jobs after multiple women came forward with stories of assault or harassment. But sexual assault and harassment usually occur in private. It's very hard to prove what really happened.

A backlash quickly accused the #MeToo movement of going too far. What if innocent men and boys were falsely accused? How could we allow men to be punished for the unproven claims of a few women? Many men feared they would be accused. Someone could lie about them, or misinterpret their behavior. Would their futures be destroyed because they patted a woman's back?

Other critics noted that some of the behavior called out by the movement was not illegal. The lines can blur when it comes to sexual behavior. Say a man pressures a woman for sex on a date, and she ultimately gives in. Is he a rapist, a jerk, or simply persuasive? If a woman says no, but doesn't leave or fight back, did she really mean no? What if a man tells sexual jokes at work, and a woman takes offense? Is he a sexual harasser, or is she too sensitive?

There are degrees to sexual harassment. Grabbing a woman's bottom is not the same as rape. If we lump everything together, it could diminish the most serious crimes. Some worry that overreacting could lead to society taking sexual assault less seriously. Policing every word and gesture could do more harm than good. We all make mistakes. Firing someone for a minor misdeed doesn't allow people to make mistakes and learn from them.

Even Burke has expressed concern that the #MeToo movement could go in the wrong direction. She worries that the movement focuses too much on popular white celebrities. The stories of women of color may be lost or ignored. She's also concerned that #MeToo focuses on sharing stories on social media. The demand that we share our traumas publicly is hard on some survivors. Announcing and reliving the trauma doesn't help people heal. Instead, she wants people to share stories of their healing.

Regardless of the complaints, the #MeToo movement has changed society in America. It is also spreading to other countries. Men who have gotten away with bad behavior for years are being called to account. A few women are also being called out for sexual harassment. Yet many more people still get away with sexual harassment on the job. Less than one percent of rapists are imprisoned for their crimes.

Can the #MeToo movement put an end to sexual violence? If nothing else, it has initiated conversations about consent. It has allowed more people to come forward with their stories. It helps victims find support and healing. Much work remains to be done. Will people lose interest in the coming years? Or will they take this as an opportunity to change society for the better, for good?

People will likely never agree on exactly how the #MeToo movement should work. They'll argue that it has gone too far, or not far enough. The questions surrounding the #MeToo movement give rise to vigorous debate. In chapters titled "Is the #MeToo Movement Good for Society?" "Has #MeToo Gone Too Far?" "Whom Should We Believe?" and "How Will the #MeToo Movement Change the Future?" *Opposing Viewpoints: The #MeToo Movement* presents viewpoints from all sides of the issues.

# CHAPTER 1

# Is the #MeToo Movement Good for Society?

# Chapter Preface

On the surface, a movement intended to reduce sexual violence must be positive. But any large political movement causes controversy. Some people fear that #MeToo is unfair to men. Innocent men and boys could be falsely accused. Sexual assault and sexual harassment are not the same, but men may be demonized for either. They might lose their jobs and reputations after telling a bad joke or being a lousy date. Could this even lead to society taking sexual assault less seriously?

The viewpoints in this chapter explore the effect the #MeToo movement has had on society in just a few short years. One viewpoint author argues that sexual harassment can lead to sexual violence. Therefore, writes the author, we should take both seriously. Even if the #MeToo movement hurts men, the cost is worthwhile if it reduces violence against women. Besides, women and minorities have lived in fear for centuries. Why shouldn't men know fear, too?

Another author claims the #MeToo movement tries to shut down any criticism. This stifles debate and prevents women and men from expressing opinions. The author argues that the movement treats women as children who cannot take care of themselves.

Another viewpoint notes some of the good things that have come from #MeToo. For example, calls to helplines have gone up, and more people have felt free to share their stories. A legal defense fund offers free help to victims who could not otherwise afford it. These signs show how #MeToo has helped society, and also how far we have yet to go.

Several viewpoint authors argue that the #MeToo movement benefits men, along with women. After all, men can be victims of sexual harassment and assault. Yet men may hesitate to come forward for fear of being seen as weak or unmanly. As more people discuss the problem, the stigma fades. In addition, men who fear accusations of sexual assault need to know how to behave. #MeToo is clarifying guidelines and teaching people about consent. That can only help men and boys who want to be good friends, coworkers, and dates. That makes schools, workplaces, and relationships safer for everyone.

> *"Sexual violence happens on a spectrum so accountability has to happen on a spectrum."*

# The Growth of the #MeToo Movement

*Emma Brockes*

*In the following viewpoint Emma Brockes discusses the months after the #MeToo movement exploded in 2017. The author reports on an interview with Tarana Burke, who first used the phrase "Me Too" much earlier. Burke discusses her work with women and girls of color who have been victims of sexual violence. She addresses some of the concerns people have about the #MeToo movement. She largely dismisses the fears that the #MeToo movement will harm men more than it helps women. Women are far more at risk of sexual violence than men are at risk of being falsely accused. Burke also argues that people should be concerned about sexual harassment as well as sexual violence. She sees one as leading to the other. Emma Brockes is a* Guardian *columnist based in New York. She is the author of* She Left Me The Gun: My Mother's Life Before Me.

"#MeToo Founder Tarana Burke: 'You Have to Use Your Privilege to Serve Other People,'" by Emma Brockes, Guardian News and Media Limited, January 15, 2018. Reprinted by permission.

As you read, consider the following questions:

1. How did the #MeToo movement start, and how did it expand greatly in 2017?
2. Why was Tarana Burke worried about the #MeToo movement going online?
3. Why does Burke feel that sexual harassment is a gateway to sexual violence?

L ast October—three months and a lifetime ago—Tarana Burke was sitting in bed, scrolling through Twitter, when some unusual activity caught her eye. The 44-year-old had 500 followers and no great taste for social media: her work with survivors of sexual violence, mainly young women of colour, didn't lend itself to public pronouncement. Twelve years earlier she had set up Me Too, an activist group that she thought, in her wildest dreams, might one day amount to a Me Too bumper sticker on somebody's car—a kind of bat signal between survivors of sexual violence—but that on most days had no public presence at all. For her kind of work to be done right, she believed, most of it needed to be done in the dark.

What she saw on Twitter therefore made Burke jump out of her skin. Ten days earlier, Harvey Weinstein had been spectacularly exposed by the *New York Times* as the subject of multiple accusations of sexual assault, and there on screen, carrying the hashtag #MeToo, other women had begun sharing their stories. Burke didn't know that the actor Alyssa Milano had stumbled on the phrase, unaware of its origins, and urged survivors of sexual aggression to use it. Nor could she know that, in the coming weeks, the Me Too hashtag would be used more than 12 million times, resulting in an extraordinary outpouring of pain, and a handful of high-profile men losing their jobs. All she knew that night was that someone was using her slogan and this wasn't good. "Social media," she says, laughing at the understatement, "is not a safe space. I thought: this is going to be a f***ing disaster."

Burke and I are in the offices of Girls for Gender Equity, a non-profit organisation in downtown Brooklyn where she is the senior director. "Congratulations Tarana!" reads a homemade poster on her office door, alongside a photocopy of *Time* magazine's Person of the Year cover, featuring the "silence breakers" of #MeToo (fruit picker Isabel Pascual, lobbyist Adama Iwu, actor Ashley Judd, software engineer Susan Fowler, Taylor Swift and an anonymous hospital worker are pictured, while Burke was honoured on the inside pages). Burke has just returned from LA after attending the Golden Globes with Michelle Williams; as she talks she is trying to eat a quesadilla from a polystyrene container while keeping an eye on her phone. This is one of the busiest times of year for the organisation, she says. "The world doesn't realise I have a regular job!"

The idea of attending the Golden Globes was a challenge. "When Michelle called me and said: 'I would love to take you to the Golden Globes,' I said: 'Why? I'm trying very hard not to be the black woman who is trotted out when you all need to validate your work.'" Ouch.

"Well, Michelle is very thoughtful and she said: 'That's not what I want to do.'" Instead, the two of them came up with the idea of "flooding the red carpet with women activists—I know some badass women activists from around the country, across the spectrum, all races and classes, different issues—and we wondered what it would look like if we used the time usually allotted to [red-carpet trivia] for our issues." There were eight activists in the end, a smaller number than they had originally wanted but a signal, she says, of "how women have historically supported each other."

It is possible that Burke's use of the term "safe space" has already annoyed you; it's a term that, like "trigger warning," "micro-aggression" and "rape culture," has come to act on some people with the force of a hostile ideology—either that or make them glaze over. Last week in Le Monde, Catherine Deneuve signed an open letter denouncing the #MeToo movement as totalitarian, and a similar piece ran in the *New York Times* grumbling that it reduced women to the level of "Victorian housewives." No one used the term snowflake, but that is the implication: that #MeToo is driven by the same people who think books should be banned and pieces of art they don't like taken down from museums.

Burke, it must be said, is not this person. She is open to criticism. She allows that in a movement so large and fast-moving there are inevitable and considerable shortcomings. "Sexual violence happens on a spectrum so accountability has to happen on a spectrum," she says. "I don't think that every single case of sexual harassment has to result in someone being fired; the consequences should vary. But we need a shift in culture so that every single instance of sexual harassment is investigated and dealt with. That's just basic common sense."

Burke's prediction that Me Too, in its latest iteration, would be a disaster was not because innocent men might suffer, or because the difference between assault and harassment might be lost, but because victims of sexual violence might be poorly served by the publicity. For two decades, Burke has done the grinding, unglamorous, financially ruinous work of setting up programmes to help victims of abuse, and that didn't tend to include sharing their status online. As it turns out, she thinks the de-stigmatising effect of #MeToo represents a greater gain than the anticipated risks, and if she is unmoved by the accusation that we are in the midst of an overcorrection, it is because she has seen what the alternative—doing nothing—looks like.

She is also aware of the numbers. At one of the first Me Too workshops Burke ran, for high school-age girls in Tuskegee, Alabama, she asked the girls to fill in a worksheet noting three things they hadn't known before they came, adding that if they needed help, they should write "Me Too" on the paper. "Doing it that way, it wasn't like: raise your hand if you want a Me Too sheet!" she says. "We weren't asking people to out themselves." At the end of the event, she and her colleague collected the sheets. "I'll never forget," says Burke. "There had been 30 or so girls in the room and we expected around five or six Me Toos." There were 20. "And we looked at these things and said: 'Oh, s**t.'"

The work that grew out of that is almost too subtle for the volatility of the current moment to bear, but it is the basis of what Burke hopes Me Too will become; use the hashtag, she says, "but let's talk about why, and let's talk about what happens after." For Burke, that means confidence-building which is to say, establishing the difference between self-esteem and self-worth. "I think a lot of girl-centred programmes are like: 'We want to build your self-esteem by telling you that you're beautiful, and asking you to tell yourself you're beautiful every single day!' That rang false to me. Because I can tell you that if you live in a world that devalues you, there is nothing to support that message. I want girls to feel worthy just for existing, because for black and brown girls—and actually just for girls—it's 'You're worthy if'; so, if you're the smartest girl, or if you're the prettiest girl, or if you run the fastest. There has to be something attached to it to add value to your life and that can become something you become consumed with—'I have to have this thing; I have to be beautiful.' So, for me, it was like, 'Let me teach you what the world thinks about us, and let me teach you what we've seen the world do to girls who look like us. And let me teach you why they're wrong.'"

Burke is, of course, not immune to the forces she is teaching the girls to resist, although, as she points out, she is also a single mother of a 20-year-old daughter and has a badass attitude and a lot of life experience. Still, when she logs on to social media and isn't quick enough to filter the comments, there it is: the thing from which all women are supposed effortlessly to move on, because to do otherwise is to be a Victorian. "Oh, every day," she says cheerfully, of being attacked by trolls. What do they say? She smiles. "They say: 'You are too ugly to rape.'"

It is possible that, thanks to #MeToo, some women who might usefully have shrugged off a minor grievance may decide to pursue it. They may—in the language of the times—internalise an idea of themselves as victims. This is the argument running counter to Me Too and it's one that, rightly I think, Burke laughs out of the room, not least because, even with the huge swell of #MeToo testimony, it is still not exactly cool to out yourself as a victim of sexual violence.

What, I ask, of the argument that there will be collateral damage and some men will be overly punished for minor transgressions? "I hate that," says Burke. "I don't want that to be true. I'm sure it will be true, just as there is a small percentage of accusations of sexual assault that are just not true. But I tend to pivot away from that because people tend to blow that up and make it the main thing; 'What if she's lying?!' OK. But it's, like, a 3% chance."

She also won't have it that sexual violence and sexual harassment are entirely unrelated things. "[People say:] 'There's sexual harassment over here and you shouldn't conflate it with rape,'" she says. "Which is true; those are two very different things. But they're on the same spectrum. Sexual harassment is like the gateway drug. It's the entry point. 'Nothing happens, so let's go a little bit further.'"

The greater threat is that Me Too is an invitation for women to whom nothing serious has happened to assume the status of victims. Burke fairly screams at this. "Of all the critiques—and I'm very open to critiques of this work—that one in particular makes me crazy. Because I think the women who are saying that don't realise what they are doing. There is inherent strength in agency. And #MeToo, in a lot of ways, is about agency. It's not about giving up your agency, it's about claiming it."

What about the temptation to overstate minor transgressions? "There was a murky time—maybe it still exists—when people would say: 'Well, this guy one time touched my boob; I don't know if I can say #MeToo.' And I'd say to people: 'I cannot define how you or your body responds to things. I can't tell you that's not trauma.' I've seen cases with young people and families where there is a child who has experienced some form of sexual violence and there is one set of parents who say: 'That's just kids experimenting.' And there are others who say: 'I'm going to get my kid into therapy, this

## #MeToo and Women's Employment

The #MeToo movement, originally started by Tarana Burke in 2006, went viral on social media in October 2017. Since then, its impact has been quantifiable, according to the Equal Employment Opportunity Commission. The Commission said it saw a 7,500 increase, or 12 percent, in harassment complaints filed from October 2017 to September 2018, compared to 2016.

But as a rising tide lifts all boats, the movement's impact trickled down to other aspects of corporate America—like hiring. New data from Boston-based recruitment marketplace provider Scout Exchange found a 41 percent spike in the number of women hired for executive roles paying more than $100,000 a year.

The study also focused on the pay gap between women and men in different sectors and found a 22 percent pay gap across job roles in engineering, human resources, clinical jobs, sales, administration and marketing. While the average salary earned by men was $110,000, for women it was $90,000.

What's interesting, however, is that the parity is higher for some of these roles than others. Sales, marketing and administration, for example, reflected a wider gap. Women professionals in marketing

is traumatic.' Some of that is based on the response of the child, and I think that happens in general. It's what you respond to."

It is also the language in which you choose to respond. "When I first started Me Too, young people had no language to talk about this," she says. "And that's something I've seen change; young people have a way to talk about it now. Hearing the words 'rape culture' doesn't seem foreign to them." You can dislike the tone of this language; you can find it aggressive, or vague, or wide-reaching, but there is no doubt that to the person drenched in shame, hearing the words "rape culture" communicates at the most basic level: it isn't your fault.

Burke has been through this experience herself; as a child, she was assaulted by some boys in her neighbourhood, and it is one of the things that motivated her to become an activist. "I roles made 73 percent of what their male counterparts did. For administrative roles, women made 83 percent compared to men. And in sales, the number was 84 percent compared to men. The smallest differences in pay were found in IT and engineering roles. Scout Exchange collected from its platform that's used by employers and recruiters over the past 18 months.

Salaries in tech might be catching up, but what about the parity in employee equity? According to a study released in September by Carta, a Palo Alto, Calif.-based company that helps startups manage employee and investor equity, female employees at startups own 47 cents for every dollar of equity a male employee owns.

Massachusetts, however, has taken the lead on closing this gap. The state's equal pay act went into effect in July this year. Shortly after, Mayor Martin J. Walsh spearheaded the Boston Women's Workforce Council initiative, which is a public-private partnership between the mayor's office and the Greater Boston business community dedicated to closing the gender pay gaps in Boston by removing visible and invisible barriers to advancement for women in the workforce.

"Is the #MeToo Movement Helping Women Get Better Jobs?" by Srividya Kalyanaraman, American City Business Journals, November 29, 2018.

grew up in, not poverty—that sounds a bit Tiny Tim—but, you know, low-income, working-class family in a housing project in the Bronx. We didn't have a ton of resources. But my mother was very determined—she had me in all sorts of programmes; anything she could put me in, she did. And I read a lot when I was young. Those were the things that helped change the trajectory of my life. And the first glimpses of healing, and understanding what had been happening to me as a child, came from the literature that I read. So I had this 'out' that I saw the girls I worked with did not have."

The process of healing is one that she would say is never complete, and part of Burke's discomfort with the spotlight—"I'm uncomfortable being the face of this thing; I didn't want to be a figurehead"—is that, she says, "I'm still dealing with my own stuff." She is squeamish about what she calls, drily, her "15 minutes," not least because people keep encouraging her to monetise it. "Ever since this went viral, people have been saying: 'You should sell Me Too T-shirts! How do I get those T-shirts?!' Everyone has a stream of income idea." (In fact, there are Me Too T-shirts that Burke has, for years, barely been able to give away. Until recently, every time she wore one out of the house, guys would read the slogan on the front and say flirtatiously: "Oh, me too! Me too!" Then they would see the back, which read something like "end sexual violence now" and Burke would wait, amused, for the terrible silence. "The guys would be like: 'Er, I'm so sorry.'" She laughs uproariously.)

Anyway, she says, "We don't sell the T-shirts because they are a gift. A lot of times I hand them out and say: 'Whenever you're ready.'"

Between *Time* magazine and the Golden Globes, Burke's profile is continuing to grow, and she is determined to rise to the demands. "Inherently, having privilege isn't bad," she says, "but it's how you use it, and you have to use it in service of other people." For what feels like the first time, the privilege she is referring to is her own, and it is the privilege of an extremely large audience. "Now that I have it, I'm trying to use it responsibly," she says. "But if it hadn't come along I would be right here, with my f***ing Me Too shirt on, doing workshops and going to rape crisis centres." She gives a huge laugh. "The work is the work."

> *"The norms and changes that the #MeToo movement seeks to put in place would likely leave us with social habits that make men less likely to be susceptible to false accusations."*

# Men Don't Need to Fear False Accusations

*Neil Van Leeuwen*

*In the following viewpoint, Neil Van Leeuwen addresses how the #MeToo movement affects men. Some people fear that girls will ruin boys' lives through false claims. The author argues that this is highly unlikely. For one thing, he doubts people will be that gullible. In addition, he believes the discussion of consent will help boys and men. If they understand consent and follow guidelines set up by #MeToo, males can avoid behavior that could lead to accusations. Neil Van Leeuwen is a philosopher of mind at Georgia State University. Philosophy Talk encourages philosophy discussions on science, religion, and culture.*

"How #MeToo Helps Men," by Neil Van Leeuwen, Philosophy Talk, October 23, 2018. Reprinted by permission.

As you read, consider the following questions:

1. Why does the author think most people won't easily believe false claims?
2. Why will getting clear consent help boys and men avoid accusations of sexual assault, according to the author?
3. How can an understanding of MeToo and consent improve the workplace for women and help men avoid false accusations?

O ne of my college friends recently posted a meme on Facebook that read:

> Every mother of boys should be TERRIFIED that at ANY time ANY girl can fabricate ANY story, with no proof, & RUIN her boy's life.

And she shared her own comment on it: "Regardless of where you stand on the Kavanaugh issue, this is the reality many of us are coming to understand." As it happens, she's the mother of three young boys. Accordingly, she must be "TERRIFIED" that inheritors of the #MeToo movement will one day vindictively "fabricate" a story ("ANY story") and "RUIN" life for one or more of her sons.

The background picture suggested by this meme is that the norms the #MeToo movement seeks to put in place will come at a severe cost to men. The implicit thought behind this picture— be it disingenuous or not—is easy to grasp: if society's default is to believe women who claim they were sexually assaulted, that will open men up to rampant false accusations, which women (thinly veiled subtext: women like Christine Blasey Ford) will exploit for malicious purposes. There is even a #ProtectOurBoys movement dedicated to boosting that thought. In short, on this picture, because of #MeToo, men in the 21st century will be as susceptible to false accusations of sexual assault as Black men were in America for most of the 20th century.

That thought gets a lot of things wrong. First, it overestimates the likely rates of false accusations, which are at present very low. Second, it overestimates the gullibility of those in the future who would hear the "fabricated" accusations. Would people really believe "ANY" story from "ANY" girl at "ANY" time? According to that, people would believe incoherent accusations that go contrary to widely known facts. But most people aren't that gullible. In the worst case, one might err on the side of believing a plausible accusation that hasn't been proven, which is a far cry from the hysterical picture painted by the meme in question.

Those two points have been widely rehearsed in public discussion, so I don't want to expand on them here.

Rather, I want to question the zero-sum logic of the thought behind the meme itself. That logic says that any move in the direction of trusting the accusers/victims inevitably increases the possibility and likelihood of false accusations that do actual damage. And I want to address that zero-sum logic, because I think it is tacitly accepted not only by opponents of the changes #MeToo would bring about—but also by defenders. For the opponents, like my friend, that logic is a reason to reject #MeToo. For defenders, it is a cost worth bearing, given the much greater moral benefits that would come from a culture of trusting victims.

The point I want to advance here, however, is that the zero-sum logic is questionable and likely wrong. The norms and changes that the #MeToo movement seeks to put in place would likely leave us with social habits that make men less likely to be susceptible to false accusations. If so, then my friend should be happy that her boys will come of age in a post-#MeToo era.

One of the key points of #metoo and related movements is that sex requires consent and good communication generally. Boys will now grow up hearing this. Contrast that with the message I got in high school and college in the 1990s. I recall being in a nightclub in 1999 when I heard an older male advise me: "Don't ask. Just grab her and kiss her!" I'm guessing his approach to sex was not that different: don't talk first. But such a lack of verbal communication eventuates in sexual situations in which there hasn't been a decisive moment of consent. And not only are such situations likelier to actually be moments of sexual assault; they are also situations that are more susceptible to malicious characterization than are situations in which consent has been explicitly given or denied. If there has been a decisive moment of consent, then a false accusation would have no plausibility. If there has not been a decisive moment of consent, then a male following post-#MeToo norms would not attempt a sex act. Either way, the greater clarity of consent that will be normal in the post-#MeToo era will help stop males from doing things that even could be falsely construed.

My general reasoning here is that reducing the prevalence of ambiguous situations—those in which the male doesn't definitively know how willing a potential partner is—will not only reduce incidence of actual assault but also the possibility of false accusation. If we are concerned with false accusations (as my friend was), then we should want as much clarity as possible, since lies are less likely to thrive in contexts where communication has been clear.

And the point about reducing ambiguity generalizes beyond the bedroom. A big part of what #MeToo tries to do is improve professional life for women, which includes combating sexual harassment in the workplace. That involves having stricter standards of professional communication: avoid sexual jokes, flirtation, etc. unless all parties are clearly comfortable with it, and even then proceed with caution and be prepared to back off. But a male following that norm is less likely to say or do something that could be wrongly construed as harassment. So that means that the norm that #MeToo supports for the workplace will reduce the kind of ambiguous situation that even could provide fodder for a false accusation. So this norm, in point of fact, helps men: follow the norm and be less susceptible to false accusation. (And again, keep in mind that I'm not saying false accusations are all that likely in the first place; I'm saying that following #MeToo norms will make males even less susceptible to them, however likely they may be.)

There are several other ways I think #MeToo norms are helpful to men (and women in positions of power, for that matter) beyond the potential for false accusation. Better awareness of the impact of power relations on the ability to give consent, for example, will help keep supervisors from crossing into territory where they think they've been given consent but haven't been (the number of cases that that point describes is staggering).

So the general theme is clear: #MeToo norms will help males avoid being actual aggressors, help them avoid ambiguous situations that would leave them susceptible to being falsely perceived as such, and help them avoid mistaking power relations for consent. All of that is good for men. So instead of besmirching the #MeToo movement, anxious mothers of young boys should embrace it.

> "*By emphasizing consent and puncturing gender stereotypes, MeToo has the potential to help everyone, of every gender, have better sexual choices, and better sex.*"

# When Women Speak, Men Are Empowered

*Noah Berlatsky*

*In the following viewpoint, Noah Berlatsky offers another perspective on how the #MeToo movement affects men. He argues that backlash has claimed #MeToo will harm men. In reality, he says, the movement has allowed male victims to speak up. Men can be victims of sexual harassment and assault, from other men or from women. Yet they rarely come forward for fear of being seen as unmanly. The author argues that #MeToo can make both relationships and workplaces safer for everyone. It's not a battle between women and men, but rather an attempt to keep people from abusing power. Noah Berlatsky writes about gender, culture, and comics for many publications, including the* Guardian, *the* Atlantic, *and the* Washington Post.

"Dear Men, #Metoo Isn't Trying to Silence You. It's Trying to Empower You," by Noah Berlatsky, Quartz Media LLC, January 19, 2018. Reprinted by permission.

As you read, consider the following questions:

1. What percentage of men are victims of sexual violence?
2. Why are male victims of sexual harassment and violence sometimes left out of the conversation?
3. How do stereotypes about the ways men and women feel about sex hurt both men and women?

The #MeToo backlash is upon us. There's already been a contingent of men and women worrying about "witch hunts" and overcorrections. Now, in the wake of a controversial article accusing Hollywood star Aziz Ansari of sexual misconduct, the idea that the movement has gone too far is gaining momentum. "Apparently there is a whole country full of young women who don't know how to call a cab, and who have spent a lot of time picking out pretty outfits for dates they hoped would be nights to remember. They're angry and temporarily powerful," Caitlin Flanagan writes in an article for the *Atlantic*, dismissing the allegations against Ansari.

This kind of worldview assumes that men and women are locked in a Battle of the Sexes. If women are suddenly empowered, men suffer.

But the truth is that the interests of men and women are aligned. While women are disproportionately singled out for sexual violence and harassment, #MeToo has shown that men can be victims too, and that disproportions of power can lead to harassment of men as well as women. The evidence of #MeToo doesn't show that women need to triumph over men. Rather, it shows that a world in which sexual abuse and workplace harassment are not tolerated, and in which a respectful approach to consensual, mutually pleasurable sex is the norm, is a better world for men and women both.

Male victims are often let out of #MeToo conversations, in part this is because there are fewer of them. But male victims are also erased because men are not supposed to be victims. Instead, men are supposed to be strong and powerful—which means identifying with sexual aggressors or, more positively, identifying as defenders of women.

This is why politicians who condemn sexual violence often preface their denunciations by identifying themselves as "a father of daughters." Men are supposed to imagine themselves racing to the defense of the women in their care. They're not supposed to identify directly with the victim, because that would make them look weak. A male politician getting up in the public sphere and referencing his own experience of workplace harassment, or his own sexual abuse, is almost unthinkable.

And yet men account for between 5% and 38% of victims of sexual violence—the exact numbers vary so widely because men are often unwilling to report sexual assaults. Despite that reluctance, many male victims have come forward in the last few months during #MeToo. Fifteen men accused Kevin Spacey of sexual harassment, including actor Anthony Rapp, who says Spacey made sexual advances to him when he was 14. Terry Crews, an ex-football player, and nobody's image of a typical victim, says a Hollywood agent groped him in 2016. *Former Star Trek* actor George Takei was accused of sexually assaulting a male model in 1981.

The people who accused Spacey and Takei weren't "out to get" men. They were men themselves. Moreover, these examples also show that #MeToo, contrary to some claims, does not cast women as perpetual victims in need of protection. On the contrary, #MeToo made space for men to come forward, demonstrating that men are not always in positions of power, and that it is not always women who are abused.

Just as men can be the victims of sexual harassment, they can also agree to unwanted sex. The #MeToo movement has highlighted the need for people to respect sexual boundaries, and obtain clear consent from partners. The stereotypical scenario here is that of a man pressuring a woman for sex. But research by Jessie Ford, a sociology PhD student at New York University, suggests that men, too, can be pushed into sex they don't want, or that they regret.

A few of the men Ford interviewed said that they had sex that they did not want when they were drunk. Most, however, said that they felt that they had to accept sex if a woman offered, because otherwise they would be perceived as emasculated or homosexual. "There is this social pressure that men like sex a lot and women can choose yes or no. So I guess it makes you unmanly if you don't want to have sex," one of Ford's interviewees explained.

The idea that women are reluctant to have sex and need to be pushed excuses male harassers, who see any sign of resistance as a barrier to be overcome. But these gendered stereotypes also hurt men, who feel that they always have to say "yes" to sex, even when they don't want to. By emphasizing consent and puncturing gender stereotypes, MeToo has the potential to help everyone, of every gender, have better sexual choices, and better sex.

MeToo can also help everyone have better, safer workplaces. People who engage in workplace sexual harassment are often willing to violate other boundaries as well. For instance, people with a history of sexual harassment are also more likely to falsify expense reports and to take credit for other people's work.

Harvey Weinstein's horrific history of sexual abuse was part of a larger environment of bullying and mental cruelty that affected everyone at his company, Miramax. The Guardian interviewed Jesse Berdinka, a former US marine, who developed a drinking problem from the extreme stress of working with Weinstein. Workers said the environment at Miramax was like a "cult"; one said that Weinstein threw a picture frame at her during an argument.

Weinstein singled women out for sexual abuse, but he abused everyone. In forcing Weinstein out of his job, MeToo protected both women and men from a toxic workplace environment. And ideally, an increased willingness to hold powerful men (and not just men) accountable will make it easier for people to come forward about other kinds of workplace conduct as well as about sexual harassment.

"One-way conversations go down about as well with most men as they do with most women, and #MeToo isn't going to succeed in the long run if the underlying message is #STFU," Bret Stephens declared at the *New York Times*. The assumption there is that #MeToo is about women winning the Battle of the Sexes, and forcing men to cower in the corner in silence.

But empowering people to speak out against injustices is only a threat to men if you believe that men are never victims of injustice; that they never experience sexual violence, or workplace violence, or unwanted sexual pressure. As a movement, #MeToo isn't silencing men. It's showing that when women speak, men are empowered too.

> "*Sexual harassment and assault are not about love, or romance. They aren't even about sex and sexual desire. The various manifestations of sexism are about power.*"

# A Revolution of Empathy

*Jamila Rizvi*

*In the following viewpoint, Jamila Rizvi explores some of the conversations around the #MeToo movement. She argues that our culture is renegotiating the sexual contract. #MeToo has brought up questions about what counts as sexual harassment, sexual assault, or simply inappropriate behavior. Women and minorities have lived in fear for centuries. Now men are experiencing some of that fear because they don't know what's appropriate. If they use this as a time to find empathy and compassion, they can help themselves and others. Jamila Rizvi is an author and political commentator. Her book,* Not Just Lucky, *explores how low confidence can hurt women in their careers.*

"In a Post #Metoo World, Bravery and Empathy Are One and the Same," by Jamila Rizvi, Nine Digital Pty Ltd, August 15, 2018. Reprinted by permission.

As you read, consider the following questions:

1. How has the #MeToo movement led to a new negotiation of the sexual contract, according to the author?
2. Why do women sometimes fear saying no to a man, according to the article?
3. Why should men think about women's experiences, according to the author?

Following the initial blanket media coverage of Hollywood's #MeToo moment, the conversation threatened to rebound in multiple, unexpected directions. Like an AFL footy, the bounce was hard to predict.

We wondered who would be next; partially concerned for the victims but mostly just sucked in by a perverse form of voyeurism.

The "who next?" line of inquiry quickly gave way to a tsunami of opinion pieces asking, "What counts and what doesn't?"

Public chatter became increasingly confused by accusations that moved beyond the broadly-accepted definition of sexual assault, to include a variety of—not criminal, but—inappropriate and sexist workplace behaviours.

Author and commentator Masha Gessen wrote in the *New Yorker* that our society may be renegotiating the sexual contract.

This kind of discussion isn't new, Gessen explains, but something human beings have done at many points in history.

A point of so-called sexual reckoning isn't original—it's simply the next shift in the always evolving rules and customs that govern physical and social interaction.

Indeed, the discussion around #MeToo has largely happened alongside the legal system, rather than forming a critique of the law itself.

This is a debate around culture. A culture of cover-up, a culture where women aren't believed, a culture that says men can do as they wish because "boys will be boys" and "he was just trying to be friendly."

Cultural lines are harder to re-draw than legal ones. They're dotted and wiggly, not bold and decisive.

Responding to accusations that men are now afraid and confused by what is and isn't appropriate workplace behaviour, feminist author Jessica Valenti is unmoved.

She said on Twitter that a little fear on the part of men might actually be a good thing.

Women, she explains, are afraid every day. And she's right.

For men to take time to reconsider and reflect on their own behaviour in workplaces is a constructive step forward.

For them to really think about how their conscious—and unconscious—actions make others' feel isn't an admission of wrongdoing but an appropriate and long overdue act of compassion.

It is complex and nuanced and, as Gessen calls it, a much-needed renegotiation of the sexual contract.

Sexual harassment and assault are not about love, or romance.

They aren't even about sex and sexual desire. The various manifestations of sexism are about power.

And to my mind, that is where the much desired "line" can be drawn between what is appropriate and what isn't.

For those men seeking guidance for their own behaviour, the question you need to ask yourself is whether your behaviour is motivated by power or empathy.

A situation where a man propositions a woman and she can freely refuse—without fear of repercussions—is not the reality we inhabit.

Saying, "No thanks, mate" has consequences, and even if it doesn't, the woman has a reasonable fear that it might.

Girls and women are still taught to let men down gently, to cushion their egos, to protect themselves in their decline of another's advance.

In a recent episode of the ABC's *Conversation Hour,* Richard Fidler interviewed writer Rick Morton, who spoke about the fear of being found out as gay in a small country town and being abused.

The abuse, which happened a handful of times, wasn't what broke his spirit. It was the ever-present fear that it would, during all those days it did not.

Learning to live with fear is what women and minorities have done for centuries and it has caused damage.

The lesson here is that in making an approach to a woman, men need to exercise empathy.

Consider her position, her anxieties, and how they have been shaped by lived experience quite different from your own.

Consider whether she will feel pressured to give an answer that she doesn't want to give and amend your own behaviour accordingly.

Consider the world from her point of view. Don't put a proposition in such a way that maximises her chances of saying yes, but in such a way that maximises her opportunity to respond in accordance with her own desires.

By calling a woman colleague "darling," are you really doing her a kindness? Or is it an unconscious reaffirmation that your status is higher than hers?

When you kiss a woman on the cheek in greeting and shake the hand of a man, is it an outdated custom or simply a show of warmth and esteem?

Of course, it's possible that it can be both.

How does it feel for her? For one woman colleague it might be a demonstration of friendship, while another might be quite uncomfortable.

Empathy requires you to consider the feelings of both as individuals and act accordingly.

You wouldn't swear in front of your mum the way you do when you're with your mates, so why not adapt your behaviour in the same way in the work context as well?

Accordingly, this is why unequal power relations between a boss and a junior require an additional level of professionalism and care.

Someone who is a subordinate necessarily wields substantially less power, meaning an interaction is more likely to be about that power and less likely to be about empathy.

Interrogating your own behaviour and the various—often unseen—ways it might make others feel is the key.

In fact, "empowerment through empathy" was the motto chosen by activist Tarana Burke, the original founder of the #MeToo movement.

Author of the now infamous Media Men List, Moira Donegan writes for *The Cut* that: "We're being challenged to imagine how we would prefer things to be.

"This feat of imagination is about not a prescriptive dictation of acceptable sexual behaviors but the desire for a kinder, more respectful, and more equitable world.

"There is something that's changed: Suddenly, men have to think about women, our inner lives and experiences of their own behavior, quite a bit. That may be one step in the right direction."

If Masha Gessen is right and we are renegotiating the sexual contract, then we have only just begun.

To discuss and debate these issues openly and honestly will take a new kind of bravery.

Bravery is a concept that for as long as humans have had language was defined in typically male terms. That is no longer the case. To be empathetic is to be brave.

To think about someone else's needs, feelings, experiences and to set those, if not above, then at least as equal to our own, currently constitutes a revolutionary act.

And damn, if that revolution isn't well overdue.

> "*MeToo is a moral crusade where facts are readily sacrificed for the greater good of the cause.*"

# The #MeToo Movement Treats Women Like Children

*Joanna Williams*

*In the following viewpoint, Joanna Williams explores reasons to be concerned about the #MeToo movement. She says the movement is intolerant of criticism, which stops debate. This can demonize women who don't behave in the way the movement wants. The author claims that #MeToo cares less about provable facts and more about the feelings of the accusers. She argues that the movement treats women like children who need protection. She is concerned that #MeToo is doing damage and says the movement should be challenged. Joanna Williams is the author of* Women vs. Feminism: Why We All Need Liberating from the Gender Wars. *The American Conservative is a nonprofit organization devoted to conservative values.*

"Six Months in, #MeToo Has Become Infantilizing and Authoritarian," by Joanna Williams, the American Conservative, April 19, 2018. Reprinted by permission.

As you read, consider the following questions:

1. How has unwanted behavior become associated with sexual misconduct, according to the author?
2. How has #MeToo put some women out of work, according to the article?
3. How does the movement treat women like children, according to the author?

It's six months since #MeToo began trending on social media. Since then, those two little words have sparked a conversation about the sexual harassment of women that has spread across the globe and into every walk of life. Half a year on it's time to take stock and ask what women have gained from this movement.

The accusations made against Harvey Weinstein by numerous actors and employees and reaching back over decades are by now skin-crawlingly familiar. Yet the *New York Times* story in which actress Ashley Judd and others first publicly detailed Weinstein's alleged sexual misconduct, leading to his resignation just three days later, could have made headlines for a week and then been consigned to history. Instead, the story continued apace and the list of victims—and those accused—grew.

One week later, actress Alyssa Milano tweeted: "If you've been sexually harassed or assaulted write 'me too' as a reply to this tweet." Milano hadn't realized she was employing a phrase first coined by activist Tarana Burke as a means of offering solidarity to women victims of sexual violence. More than a decade later, and with celebrity backing, #MeToo spread rapidly to become a global movement that extended far beyond social media.

Joining in with #MeToo is an attractive proposition. Women sharing their stories become part of a community (albeit one that exists more in their imagination than in reality); they gain validation for their suffering and the moral beatification afforded to innocent victims. Significantly, #MeToo doesn't appear to be about women wallowing in victimhood; on the contrary, it seems

# An Unintended Shift

One year ago Alyssa Milano, an American actress, posted on Twitter: "If you've been sexually harassed or assaulted write 'me too' as a reply to this tweet." Within 24 hours she had received more than 500,000 responses using the hashtag "#MeToo." Ms Milano's tweet came days after the *New York Times* and *New Yorker* had published detailed allegations of sexual harassment by Harvey Weinstein, a Hollywood producer. Mr Weinstein was the first in a long line of prominent entertainers and executives to be toppled by such investigations, which dominated the headlines throughout late 2017.

Even as these stories broke, it was #MeToo that resonated most on social media, as millions of women shared their experiences of abuse, intimidation and discrimination.

Yet surveys suggest that this year-long storm of allegations, confessions and firings has actually made Americans more sceptical about sexual harassment. In the first week of November 2017, YouGov polled 1,500 Americans about their attitudes on the matter, on behalf of The Economist. In the final week of September 2018, it conducted a similar poll again. When it came to questions about

empowering. The more high-profile men that were accused, found guilty following trial by social media, and left with livelihoods and reputations ruined, the more the #MeToo movement grew emboldened.

No doubt some men have abused the power they held over women: they should be tried in a court of law and, if found guilty, punished accordingly. But those of us seriously concerned about women's rights need to move beyond the euphoria of belonging to a powerful movement and honestly appraise the impact of #MeToo. When we do, we find a number of reasons to be concerned.

#MeToo has become an orthodoxy intolerant of criticism or even question. Women who have suggested that it may have gone too far, that conflating rape with crude flirtation risks trivializing serious incidents and falsely demonizing innocent men, have been the consequences of sexual assault and misconduct, there was a small but clear shift against victims.

The share of American adults responding that men who sexually harassed women at work 20 years ago should keep their jobs has risen from 28% to 36%. The proportion who think that women who complain about sexual harassment cause more problems than they solve has grown from 29% to 31%. And 18% of Americans now think that false accusations of sexual assault are a bigger problem than attacks that go unreported or unpunished, compared with 13% in November last year. (According to the National Sexual Violence Resource Centre, an American non-profit organisation, 63% of sexual assaults are not reported to police, whereas between 2% and 10% of assault cases are falsely reported.)

Surprisingly, these changes in opinion against victims have been slightly stronger among women than men. Rather than breaking along gendered lines, the #MeToo divide increasingly appears to be a partisan one. On each of these three questions, the gap between Trump and Clinton voters is at least six times greater than the one between genders.

**"After a Year of #MeToo, American Opinion Has Shifted Against Victims," The Economist Newspaper Limited, October 15, 2018.**

hounded for thought crimes. Katie Roiphe prompted outrage when it was rumored she might go public with a list of "shitty media men" that had been widely circulated among writers and journalists. Roiphe recalls that "Before the piece was even finished, let alone published, people were calling me 'pro-rape,' 'human scum,' a 'harridan,' a 'monster out of Stephen King's "IT"' a 'ghoul,' a 'bitch,' and a 'garbage person.'" Catherine Deneuve and over 100 other prominent French women were met with a similar tsunami of name-calling and criticism following their public letter comparing #MeToo to a witch hunt. The result has been a censorious closing down of debate through a crude division between "good women" who stick to the #MeToo script and "bad women" who digress.

Criticism of the wrong kind of women respects no limits. Film producer Jill Messick, best known for her work on *Mean Girls* and *Frida*, committed suicide in February. Messick worked for Weinstein's Miramax between 1997 and 2003 and was manager for Rose McGowan in the late 1990s. As #MeToo gained ground, McGowan alleged she was raped by Weinstein and that Messick knew but did not take appropriate action. Messick was reportedly already suffering from depression; it seems unlikely that finding herself caught between McGowan and Weinstein, between claim and counterclaim, can have done much good for her mental health. The speed with which Messick was written out of history makes clear that to the #MeToo activists, some people's lives are worth more than others.

#MeToo is a moral crusade where facts are readily sacrificed for the greater good of the cause. When it comes to declaring rape, sexual assault, or harassment, what matters to activists is not objective evidence that can be proved or disproved but the subjective feelings of the accuser. #MeToo has redefined sexual misconduct as unwanted behavior. As the case against actor Aziz Ansari showed, defining abuse as unwanted behavior takes us into the realm of the bad date. Leaving a restaurant too early, pouring wine without asking, even attempting a kiss might all be considered rude, but they are only violations in the mind of the most zealous #MeToo crusaders. Women in such scenarios are robbed of all agency; apparently unable to say no, they are forced to rely on men's presumed mind-reading skills to protect them from the unwanted. Not only does this pave the way for miscarriages of justice, it makes all interactions between men and women inherently risky.

It's perhaps not surprising, then, that since #MeToo took off, surveys have suggested that men feel uncomfortable mentoring women or working alone with them at the office. As a result, women's opportunities for promotion may have been set back. And those women are lucky to have employment at all: thanks to concerns raised under the banner of #MeToo, women who worked as Formula 1 "grid girls" have lost their jobs entirely. Putting women out of work they enjoy is now a feminist act. New York waitresses were, fortunately, having none of it when a group of Hollywood actresses began petitioning for an end to the restaurant tipping culture. "Shut up!" came back their clear response.

The #MeToo movement treats women like children, incapable of ever standing up for themselves or being able to make their own choices in life. In the UK there have been calls for the street harassment of women—whistling and catcalling—to be made a criminal offense. Last week, the Screen Actors Guild proposed a ban on "hotel auditions." Its advice to women was that if a "safe venue" cannot be found for auditions then they should be accompanied by a "support peer." We need to ditch the therapeutic language and call this what it is: a chaperone. Previous generations of feminists fought against such infantilizing protections. Today's #MeToo activists are all too happy to see men demonized and women protected.

Six months on we can see that some women have certainly gained a louder voice thanks to the #MeToo movement. Sadly, all they can do with it is proclaim their own victimhood and demand greater protection. #MeToo, with its constant reiteration of outdated tropes of predatory men and vulnerable women, represents a major incursion into our personal freedoms. We need to challenge this crusade before it does any more damage.

> *"What's different for the millions of ordinary people who shared their own #MeToo stories?"*

# #MeToo Is Making Progress, Slowly

*Rebecca Seales*

*In the following article, Rebecca Seales explores the effects of the #MeToo movement. She notes that Hollywood professionals funded legal defense for people in need. Calls to a US crisis hotline rose. However, some abuse survivors found the attention given to the #MeToo movement stressful. A men's social activism group has also had more interest. In Britain, the movement seems to have affected some industries but not others. Awareness is spreading around the world, but the response varies by country. The movement has started something important, the author argues, but it may be only a first step. Rebecca Seales is a reporter for BBC News in the United Kingdom.*

As you read, consider the following questions:

1. How has the #MeToo movement helped low-wage workers who have suffered from sexual harassment?
2. What are some ways abuse survivors have responded to #MeToo?
3. Has the #MeToo movement spread to other countries? Why or why not?

"What Has #MeToo Actually Changed?" by Rebecca Seales, BBC News, May 12, 2018. First appeared in BBC News website © BBC News. Reprinted by permission.

Of course it's down to #MeToo, the campaign against sexual harassment and abuse that swept through Hollywood last autumn and has since been Googled in every country on Earth.

In its current form, the movement began with film executive Harvey Weinstein—or rather, with the dozens of women who accuse him of sexual harassment, abuse or rape. The *New York Times* printed the first allegations on 5 October, and the mogul was fired from his own company inside a week. Pandora's box was open. Harvey Weinstein denies engaging in non-consensual sex.

On 15 October, actress Alyssa Milano suggested on Twitter that anyone who had been "sexually harassed or assaulted" should reply to her Tweet with "Me Too," to demonstrate the scale of the problem. Half a million people responded in the first 24 hours.

A barrage of allegations has since emerged against high-profile men in entertainment, the media, politics, and tech. Many deny any wrongdoing. The repercussions are still in flux, but Hollywood's power dynamics have undoubtedly shifted.

That's less obviously true in the world beyond, and begs the question: What's different for the millions of ordinary people who shared their own #MeToo stories? Are the currents of the movement visible in their lives too? How far has the rallying cry been converted into real-world change?

## Testing "Time's Up": Who's Been Helped by Those Hollywood Millions?

One initiative has made solid progress (and spent solid millions) in a bid to make things better on the ground: the Time's Up Legal Defense Fund.

More than 300 actresses, writers and directors launched the project on 1 January, raising $21m (£15m) in just a month to fund legal assistance for people who suffer harassment, abuse or assault at work.

The National Women's Law Center (NWLC) in Washington DC is fielding the considerable admin, matching applicants with lawyers who can offer them free advice.

"We have received more than 2,700 requests for assistance from every state in the United States, and there are more than 500 attorneys in the network who are ready to take on Time's Up cases," Sharyn Tejani, director of the fund at the NWLC, told the BBC.

"The fund prioritises cases involving low-wage workers, women in non-traditional jobs, people of colour, LGBTQ people, and people facing legal retaliation because they dared to speak out about sexual harassment," said Ms Tejani.

Tina Tchen, who jointly leads the fund's legal aid efforts, said the beneficiaries include "construction workers, prison guards [and] police officers," adding: "There are men who have come forward too. There are some men who have experienced sexual harassment, and then there are some men who are calling, for example, on behalf of their wives or loved ones."

That's unlikely to raise surprise in some quarters. Sian Brooke of the Oxford Internet Institute, who studies gender and sexism online, says the fact that men are often victims of sexual violence was one of the most powerful takeaways from #MeToo.

"One group can be given attention and be taken seriously with regards to allegations of rape, without it taking any of the severity or weight away from another part of it," she notes.

## Has #MeToo Helped Abuse Survivors Seek Support?

From October to December 2017, calls to the Rape, Abuse & Incest National Network—a US crisis hotline—rose by 23% compared with the same period in 2016.

Some abuse survivors have cited #MeToo as a stressful influence, saying it resurfaced the pain of their abuse. Others have reported feeling less alone, saying it encouraged them to address past trauma by talking to loved ones, counsellors, or people with similar experiences.

"It's brought the idea of sexual harassment and assault into the public consciousness," Ms Brooke says. "Even if the discussion around the movement is criticism, you are still bringing about an awareness that this happens."

1in6 is a Los Angeles-based non-profit group that supports male sex abuse survivors. The group's development and communications director Meredith Alling told the BBC that #MeToo had a rapid, measurable impact on the number of men reaching out to them when the hashtag first went viral.

"We saw a 110% increase in web traffic and a 103% increase in the use of our online helpline service between September and October 2017, and the trend has continued," she said.

## What's Being Done to Create Better Workplaces?

In the US, employers are considering how best to create a positive workplace culture in the wake of #MeToo.

Ted Bunch is a co-founder of A Call To Men, a social activism group that promotes healthy, respectful ways of "being a man," and says the group has noticed an increase in enquiries.

"Most notably, we have seen an increase in corporations seeking to understand why sexual harassment in the workplace is so pervasive," he says.

Mr Bunch believes problems can arise because the workplace is a microcosm of society, in which men and boys are sometimes taught to view women as objects, and of less value than men.

"Most men are not abusive," he says, "but nearly all men have laughed at a sexist joke or objectified a woman in some way. Once you connect the dots and show men how the jokes they see as harmless actually validate and fuel more harmful behaviour, they are quick to change."

Has the push to ditch bad work cultures spread beyond the US? One British human resources consultant said she had been surprised by the lack of #MeToo-inspired queries.

"We haven't seen any spikes in the volume of training requests, or the volume of training we're recommending. I don't think it's had a significant impact," said Elaine Howell, HR manager at PlusHR.

"We have clients in professional services, manufacturing clients, financial, marketing … It appears to be quite specific to that industry [entertainment]."

Speak to Equity, the 43,000-strong British actors' union, and it's clear they've had a different experience. The union won't give exact figures, but says it's witnessed a "significant increase in enquiries and case work since #MeToo".

Vice president Maureen Beattie will take on Equity's presidency this summer, and she's keen to get the message out: toxic behaviour will not go unpunished. Or as she puts it, "If you do something to one of our members which is wrong, unacceptable, we're going to come after you. And we will come after you big-time."

"These people haven't gone away," she says. "They are under a stone. They are lurking, just waiting for the time they think nobody's looking any more.

"One of the things we're doing is asking people who have been in the business for a long time, people who are stars, people who have clout, to keep an eye out. Not that they have to be trained up in how to help somebody who's been sexually harassed, but [they] can say—with impunity and no danger of never being worked with again—'Excuse me? You can't behave like that with people.'"

## How Does an Online Movement Secure an Offline Legacy?

The #MeToo most of us know is still a new-ish creation. But it had a life before the viral hashtag. In 2006, black activist Tarana Burke founded the movement as an initiative to unite survivors of sexual violence.

Since it morphed from a low-key project into a global byword, she has embraced #MeToo's A-List flag-bearers—but her focus is on lasting change at all levels of society.

One of her most telling remarks came the week before she walked the red carpet at the 2017 Oscars: "If we keep on 'making statements' and not really doing the work, we are going to be in trouble."

Sarah J Jackson, a professor of communication studies at Northeastern University, believes context is the key to anchoring Me Too.

"I wouldn't call hashtag 'Me Too' a movement at all," she says. "I would call it a campaign that is part of a larger movement. So I would call women's rights the movement, and feminism the movement. And I would say #MeToo is one indication of the sort of conversations that need to happen.

"The next step is, OK so now we know the problem—how do we as a global community expand this conversation?"

Through its "Me Too Rising" project, Google has charted how awareness spread around the world. While data shows the term has been searched for in every corner of the planet, its resonance has inevitably been greater in some countries than others. The freedom of a nation's press and social media can certainly have impact on that—and it's too soon to tell how the movement will shape countries where it's gained traction more slowly—Japan and South Korea, for example.

Karuna Nundy, a prominent lawyer in India's Supreme Court, shared her view on #MeToo's relevance to India, where outrage over sex crimes has sparked waves of public protests in recent years.

"The #MeToo conversations in India are limited to a swathe of English-speaking, internet-enabled people. It's quite a lot in absolute numbers, but small for India. It's added, though, to the huge conversations that were already happening. The idea that due process is failing women, and civil disobedience can be legitimate."

Ms Nundy, who helped draft India's tougher anti-rape law in 2013, says victims are now more likely to be believed.

"I had a rape case yesterday against a leading Bollywood producer. My client is a very young woman; we told the court that she was raped over a period of six months on pain of bodily harm. Regardless of what the court decides, I think the way we were heard by the chief justice of the Supreme Court and the two judges is very different from the way we would have been heard, say, 15 years ago.

"There's an interplay between public consciousness, and the law and due process. And that's exactly what I think is happening."

Perhaps, then, #MeToo is not an endgame—but a clarion call to something bigger. A reminder for people to seek change in their communities, and push to make damaging systems better—especially for those who lack the power to fight alone.

# Periodical and Internet Sources Bibliography

*The following articles have been selected to supplement the diverse views presented in this chapter.*

Van Badham, "That's Patriarchy: How Female Sexual Liberation Led to Male Sexual Entitlement," the *Guardian*, Feb. 2, 2018. https://www.theguardian.com/commentisfree/2018/feb/02/thats-patriarchy-how-female-sexual-liberation-led-to-male-sexual-entitlement.

Peter Dreier, "The #MeToo Movement's Roots in Women Workers' Rights," Waging Nonviolence, Oct. 16, 2018. https://wagingnonviolence.org/feature/the-metoo-movements-roots-in-women-workers-rights/.

Srividya Kalyanaraman, "Is the #MeToo Movement Helping Women Get Better Jobs?" *Boston Business Journal*, Nov. 29, 2018. https://www.bizjournals.com/boston/news/2018/11/29/is-the-metoo-movement-helping-women-get-better.html.

Robert Koehler, "Trapped in 'a Man's World," CounterPunch, Nov. 20, 2017. https://www.counterpunch.org/2017/11/20/trapped-in-a-mans-world/.

Talia Lakritz, "These 15 Women Opened Up about Their Sexual Assault Experiences Thanks to the #metoo Campaign," Insider, Oct. 1, 2018. https://www.thisisinsider.com/me-too-hashtag-sexual-harassment-assault-2017-11.

Ephrat Livni, "There's a Problem at the Heart of #MeToo—Here's How to Solve It," Quartz, Oct. 14, 2018. https://qz.com/1422215/metoo-backlash-will-2019-be-the-year-of-men/.

Barbara Muhumuza, "All of Us: The Insidious Ways That the Patriarchy Harms Everyone," Wear Your Voice, Oct. 24, 2017. https://wearyourvoicemag.com/identities/feminism/us-insidious-ways-patriarchy-harms-everyone.

Hal Plotkin, "#MeToo—It Doesn't Only Happen to Women," Medium, Oct. 22, 2017. https://medium.com/@hplotkin/metoo-it-doesnt-only-happen-to-women-65f0d1f7e91b.

Michelle V. Rafter, "HR Responds to the #MeToo Movement," Workforce, Apr 3, 2018. https://www.workforce.com/2018/04/03/hr-responds-metoo-movement-2/.

Roger Ricketts, "#MeToo and Human Liberation," Open Democracy, Nov. 5, 2018. https://www.opendemocracy.net/rodger-ricketts/ metoo-and-human-liberation.

Jamila Rizvi, "In a Post #MeToo World, Bravery and Empathy Are One and the Same," Honey, Aug. 15, 2017. https://honey.nine. com.au/2018/08/15/17/23/metoo-movement-society-impacts.

Amanda Taub, "#MeToo Paradox: Movement Topples the Powerful, Not the Ordinary," *New York Times*, Feb. 11, 2019. https://www. nytimes.com/2019/02/11/world/americas/metoo-ocar-arias.html.

Jia Tolentino, "The Rising Pressure of the #MeToo Backlash," *New Yorker*, Jan. 24, 2018. https://www.newyorker.com/culture/ culture-desk/the-rising-pressure-of-the-metoo-backlash.

OPPOSING
VIEWPOINTS®
SERIES

# CHAPTER 2

# Has #MeToo Gone Too Far?

# Chapter Preface

\# MeToo has changed society in America. Are those changes all good, all bad, or mixed? Has the movement gone too far? In one of the viewpoints in this chapter, an author notes a downside to strict policies against sexual harassment: They make men afraid to be alone with women at work. That keeps women from networking or finding male mentors in the workplace.

#MeToo has caused some men in power to lose their jobs. Some of these men were clearly guilty of serious crimes. Most people agree that those men deserved their fates. Many would argue that the worst offenders got off too easily. Some of the most high-profile offenders returned to their careers only a few months after a weak apology. Others have continued to lay low, perhaps hoping the whole movement will blow over. But in other cases, accusations have not been proven.

The law says people are innocent until proven guilty. However, it may not be worthwhile to try sexual harassment in court. Even sexual assault can be hard to prove. Often the victims suffer more than the accused. Companies don't have to wait for proof to fire someone. Fans don't necessarily need proof before turning against celebrities. Is it fair to try people in the court of public opinion? Should someone lose their career based on one or two accusations? How many should it take? What if their behavior was rude or mean, but not illegal? Do men deserve to be punished for any poor behavior?

The following viewpoints argue whether the #MeToo movement has gone too far, or whether it should go farther. In this chapter, one viewpoint author believes we should slow down and be more careful about making and believing accusations. Other authors say we should take this opportunity to discuss the nuances around sexual harassment. An imbalance of power between men and women leads to rape culture and sexual violence. Therefore, we should address the sexism and power imbalances in society. Men should be expected to understand and care about women's feelings. They need to recognize the consequences of their actions. If they want to be forgiven for their misdeeds, they must earn forgiveness.

Most women and men want a world where sexual harassment and assault are not problems. Will the #MeToo movement help us get there? The viewpoints in this chapter debate the issue.

| "Where do we draw the line between criminality and clumsy attempts at courtship?"

# #MeToo Needs to Slow Down and Wait for Due Process

*Vinay Menon*

*In the following viewpoint, Vinay Menon looks at some of the effects of #MeToo. He notes that at first, the movement got rid of serious offenders. Later, he argues, men suffered after weaker accusations. Comedian and actor Aziz Ansari was publicly shamed for pressuring a date to have sex. Other accusations cannot be proven and may be false. The law says people are innocent until proven guilty. Therefore, the author argues, it is not fair to try people in the court of public opinion. Yet the accused are not getting due process, a fair trial by the law. The author cautions people to slow down and be more careful about accusations. Vinay Menon is a columnist and feature writer for the* Toronto Star. *He covers popular culture.*

"#MeToo Won't Last if It Isn't Fair," by Vinay Menon, *Toronto Star*, December 30, 2018. Reprinted by permission.

As you read, consider the following questions:

1. What changed after the opening months of the #MeToo movement, according to the author?
2. Has the #MeToo movement had positive effects, according to the author?
3. What are the risks of taking the movement too far, according to the author?

What is the future of #MeToo?

As we mothball 2018, the social movement remains a cultural force, one that has reshaped attitudes, fortified HR policies and placed bullhorns in the hands of sexual-abuse victims. Many men who once traipsed the corridors of power are now living ghosts, stripped of their careers and reputations, banished to purgatory.

In the last three months of 2017, as allegations of sexual misconduct gripped the news cycle almost daily, #MeToo was hailed as a seismic event, a watershed, a reckoning, a point from which there was no return.

Those last three months of 2017 felt like a mass exorcism.

We were purging demons.

But one year later, #MeToo feels #MoreComplicated. The clear-cut narratives are increasingly blurry and prone to subjective reading.

In 2017, the movement was a runaway train across a black-and-white prairie. Anyone who heard the shocking allegations against Harvey Weinstein left with one takeaway: he was a monster. There were no heated debates about Kevin Spacey or Matt Lauer, no tears for Charlie Rose or Gilbert Rozon.

The alleged misdeeds were unambiguous.

By contrast, the movement is now a hot-air balloon in a pewter sky: it is moving slower and basked in grey. This is not necessarily bad. It might even be good. The speed of #MeToo in 2017 was unsustainable. But if the ultimate goal is to stop harassment and abuse, this year's loss in momentum is a blessing in disguise: we can now exhale and poke holes into #MeToo to make it stronger.

The first problem, which emerged with allegations against comedian Aziz Ansari in January, is that we probably need to have a conversation about what constitutes mistreatment and what is just a bad date.

In the marketplace of human sexuality, what is a toxic hard sell and what is buyer's remorse? What is transactional and what is stolen? Where do we draw the line between criminality and clumsy attempts at courtship?

Published on babe.net, the effort to put Ansari in the #MeToo rogue's gallery came from a feature that recounted in graphic detail a pseudonymous 22-year-old's date with the celebrity that "turned into the worst night of my life."

But if you read the piece, waiting for the gotcha sins, you're still waiting.

There was something about this story—the Atlantic would later dismiss it as "3,000 words of revenge porn"—that did not dovetail with the spirit and exhaustive reportage of so many 2017 investigations.

This seemed less like abuse and more like character assassination.

The same might be said of bizarre allegations against TVO's Steve Paikin the following month. Former Toronto mayoral candidate Sarah Thomson claimed Paikin propositioned her during a lunch meeting. TVO launched a probe. The charge was "not substantiated." In the words of Paikin, it was "complete fiction."

Instead of lifting the #MeToo tide, the Ansari blip muddied the waters. But with Paikin we had tumbled into a treacherous riptide: the possibility an accuser was lying. And as the year rumbled on, this became a refrain from many who denied misconduct allegations while notably still championing #MeToo: David Copperfield, Michael Douglas, Ryan Seacrest, Jamie Foxx and others.

As James Franco told Stephen Colbert in response to allegations against him in January: "The things that I heard that were on Twitter are not accurate, but I completely support people coming out and being able to have a voice because they didn't have a voice for so long."

Around the same time, 100 female writers, academics, producers and actors in France—including Catherine Deneuve—signed an open letter arguing that the movement was going too far and now posed a danger to society: "In fact, #MeToo has led to a campaign, in the press and on social media, of public accusations and indictments against individuals who, without being given a chance to respond or defend themselves, are put in the exact same category as sex offenders."

The "pendulum effect," discovered by Galileo more than 400 years ago, was underway in Europe. And the #MeToo backlash would build throughout the year, steamrolling to other corners of the world where, as the Washington Post recently noted, the movement "either fizzled or never took flight."

But while the French letter was condemned in woke parts of North America, the cautionary subtext—the need for due process—became obvious in 2018. An internal investigation cleared Seacrest. An internal investigation doomed Les Moonves. An internal investigation is now underway over Neil deGrasse Tyson.

In all three cases—exoneration, guilt and to be determined—the lesson is clear: if #MeToo is to remain a powerful force it must navigate a bedrock of the West: innocent until proven guilty. To allow that principle to be inverted in the court of public opinion is to do grave injustice to actual victims of abuse.

Any lessening in the burden of proof will also worsen gender relations and create a chilling effect in workplaces if people begin to believe, as actor Liam Neeson told a late-night TV show in Ireland this year, #MeToo is "a bit of a witch hunt."

Throughout 2018, there were stories of male managers confiding they no longer felt comfortable mentoring young females or even getting into elevators with them. This anxiety over being alone with a woman—something Chris Rock jokes about and Mike Pence lives by—is not an antidote to sexual misconduct.

It is an affront to true equality.

But this fear of being wrongly accused—which in part triggered the #HimToo movement this fall and unleashed a polarized debate around Brett Kavanaugh—became an inextricable part of #MeToo in 2018.

There can be no doubt the movement has changed the way we think. It has achieved more in 15 months than was accomplished this century. It is an undertaking that is long overdue. Sexual harassment and abuse is repugnant.

But if #MeToo is to charge full speed ahead next year it must also accept that not everything is black-and-white. Some points of no return are actually forks in the road. And, ultimately, there can be no justice without due process.

> *"It feels like we have failed to find solid ground on which to build any sort of long, lasting change."*

# We Need a Bigger Cultural Shift

*Rebecca Alifimoff*

*In the following viewpoint, Rebecca Alifimoff examines the #MeToo accusations against actor Aziz Ansari from a different angle. It's true that the accusations were not part of a pattern of regular abuse or harassment on Ansari's part, and reactions are decidedly mixed about the story told by the young woman involved. Still, the author says, the incident serves as a good starting point for important discussions. People need to have conversations about consent. They need to recognize the imbalance in power between men and women, which allows men to commit sexual violence and women to be confused about why it happens. They need to address rape culture, the social attitudes that make sexual assault and abuse normal and trivial. This is how we can improve society, she says. Rebecca Alifimoff is a writer at the* Daily Pennsylvanian, *the University of Pennsylvania's student media organization.*

"A Year After #Metoo, It Feels Like Little Has Changed," by Rebecca Alifimoff, the *Daily Pennsylvanian*, January 28, 2019. Reprinted by permission.

As you read, consider the following questions:

1. Why were the accusations against Aziz Ansari different from earlier #MeToo accusations?
2. How do those claims still bring up important points about consent and rape culture, according to the author?
3. Where should the movement go now, according to the author?

A year ago, in my very first column for The Daily Pennsylvanian, I wrote about Aziz Ansari and my views on the nascent #MeToo movement.

In the past year, I've followed the movement, first with hope, then trepidation, and finally slight waves of despair, as the movement faded from a dominant cultural phenomenon to second-rate news. In some ways, this was inevitable. Nothing, no matter how outrageous, stays shocking forever.

But mostly, it feels like the promise of the movement has dissolved into empty gestures and performative rhetoric, while the predatory men the movement outed crawl back into public life.

The Ansari story was a particular flashpoint during the waves of allegations about sexual harassment and assault that seemed to come in a never-ending flood last winter. Unlike the allegations against others named in the movement, like Harvey Weinstein, Charlie Rose, Louis CK, and Matt Lauer, the allegations against Ansari were not part of a documented pattern of workplace misconduct and harassment. Instead, it was a stand alone account about a date between two single adults that went wrong.

The Ansari piece was, and remains, a flashpoint for those who have valid critiques about how the reporting of the story was handled, and those who have concerns that it was evidence of a cultural movement running off the rails.

When I wrote about the story last year, I did so because I thought that it touched a nerve, especially for me as a woman on a college campus where hook-up culture dominates. Before, the stories revealed in #MeToo seemed important, but far removed from anything I had actually experienced. The Ansari story felt familiar and accessible, and reflected in it was the beginning of a conversation that seemed like it would go beyond the workplace and start addressing other insidious double standards that often go unremarked and unspoken when it comes to sex, consent, and gender. I wrote, "It became clear to me that there is no consensus of what the term sexual assault means, and its usage becomes an easy way to stop or deliberately confuse conversation about how we as a society approach sex, and how our attitudes about sexual relations are broken."

I was hopeful in the aftermath of the rage and pain that #MeToo had exposed, that we would move past the stasis of public conversation and deliberation. That the tired routine of doubting women and minimizing the impact that sexual assault and harassment have on their lives would be over and we could move to the more nuanced conversations I feel we so desperately need to have.

I was hopeful that what would happen next would be lasting change. I hoped that once we worked from a basic understanding of the fact that harassment and assault are, in fact, bad things, that they're crimes that have victims and require consequences, we could work out how to move forward to justice and closure. I was hopeful that the path forward would stop centering on the men who had committed transgressions—who are so often richer, more famous, and overall more powerful than the women they target, and put more focus on bringing justice to victims. Once consequences were actually put in place, we could talk about the possibility of rehabilitation and forgiveness.

I don't believe in a society that punishes all transgressors equally with a permanent proverbial scarlet A, or treats all transgressions as if they are the same. So often, discussion of rape culture fails to provide adequate solutions for how to rehabilitate men who commit crimes, but that's because we're still fighting for the genuine recognition that what these men did was, in fact, a violation.

## #MeToo Has Yet to Shift Power Imbalances

Legal processes, even if based on rights, do not really effect the serious social change to attitudes or power that real gender equity will require. We need to address the social mores and related power structures that reinforce male power and support toxic masculinity.

How can we use the current explosion of evidence and outrage to trigger the needed changes?

We are still in early days of the "new" media as social change agents. Some positives: celebratory protests at award ceremonies and the wearing of supportive signs and colours have increased media coverage and the visibility of public support. There are discussions of increased resources for legal actions against perpetrators, and for more funding support to care for victims.

But these "solutions" are similar to those being pursued in the many campaigns against domestic violence, helping survivors. While these responses are needed in the short term, we must realise that they will not drive the cultural and gendered power changes we need. If "clicktivism" replaces wider political action and campaigns for change, we go backwards.

Instead of moving us forward, the fall brought the Kavanaugh hearings—an event that seemed to confirm Marx's affirmation that history happens twice, once as tragedy and once as farce. It was like being stuck in a horrible version of Groundhog Day, where the gains of #MeToo and the Anita Hill hearings amounted to nothing.

In addition, the sold-out comeback tour of Ansari—in which none of his material address the accusations against him—the planned return to television of Matt Lauer and Charlie Rose, and the semi-stealthy return to comedy of Louis CK seem like slow reversals of the gains that the movement has made.

A year removed from what seemed like one of the most significant steps forward in the crusade for women's rights in my lifetime, it feels like we have failed to find solid ground on which to build any sort of long, lasting change. Lacking an understanding

If we are serious about the abuse of gender-based power, we must look at its causes and make structural and cultural changes. We must overcome the serious, widespread gender-biased socialisation of boys and girls, in most cases long before they reach puberty.

Basic assumptions about gender roles still create beliefs about being an acceptable boy (stand up for yourself) or girl (be nice and read people's feelings). These offer surefire paths to toxic masculinity and passive femininity.

These emerged in a recent BBC documentary, broadcast on the ABC. It showed seven-year-olds displaying very stereotypical views of preferring male over female when it came to confidence in skills and leadership. It also showed how removing school and home items that reinforced gender roles could reduce the different socialisations—in other words, it's not genetic.

Given all of that, my concern is that #MeToo and related expressions of anger are failing to fix causes that increase macho-driven gender power imbalances. This means we need real, practical solutions to bridge the gender divide and stop supporting toxic masculinity.

**"#MeToo Is Not Enough: It Has Yet to Shift the Power Imbalances That Would Bring About Gender Equality," by Eva Cox, The Conversation, March 19, 2018.**

of the basics, conversations about the grey areas of consent and the nuances and gender imbalance have been unable to materialize.

As students, we occupy the epicenter of rape culture and sexual violence. We also find ourselves at a strange point in our lives where we actually have the time to think and act boldly about the sort of world we want to work towards after Penn.

Soon we will graduate and become denizens of workplaces with prevailing cultures and unspoken norms. The habits we form here at Penn—the things we chose to expect of our friends, the organizations we decided to be a part of, the behavior we tolerate on our campus—will shape the moral compasses that guide us through our infinitely more complicated post-graduate lives. We owe it, both to ourselves and to each other, to tolerate nothing more than the best.

> *"Women won't have a safe workplace if there's no means of preventing low-level harassment without resorting to firing."*

# Small Steps Are Better for Everyone

*Olivia Goldhill*

*In the following viewpoint Olivia Goldhill addresses "zero tolerance" policies on sexual harassment. Such policies impose strict punishments. When it comes to sexual harassment, the practice might fire people for first-time and relatively minor offenses. This does not make for a better workplace, according to the viewpoint. Women could avoid accusing men because they don't want to get a man fired. Men could be afraid to associate with women at all. The sources quoted suggest different ways to handle sexual harassment. People should be able to ask someone to change their behavior when it's offensive. Serious and ongoing harassment can still be handled strictly. Olivia Goldhill reports on philosophy, psychology, and neuroscience for Quartz's science desk.*

As you read, consider the following questions:

1. How is a zero-tolerance policy against sexual harassment a problem for women?
2. Why is it difficult to separate "good guys" from "bad guys"?
3. What are the best ways of handling low-level sexual harassment in the workplace, according to the article?

In the wake of allegations against Harvey Weinstein, countless organizations have hastily insisted they have a "zero tolerance" policy on sexual harassment. "Employers must adopt a zero-tolerance policy and sack the perpetrators, however valuable to the business," wrote solicitor Camilla Palmer in The Guardian.

Zero tolerance sounds like a great idea, in theory. In practice, this simplistic approach ignores the unfortunate reality that a spectrum of acts can be classed as sexual harassment. If women worry that any offense, no matter how minor, could lead to someone losing their job, then small but troubling instances of sexual harassment could go unreported.

"The problem with zero tolerance is it's very binary," says organizational psychology expert Liane Davey. "Sexual harassment and sexual assault are not at all binary."

The concern is not that men (for it's typically men who commit sexual harassment) will face unjust punishment. Rather, it's that women won't have a safe workplace if there's no means of preventing low-level harassment without resorting to firing.

Sexual harassment includes sexual invitations, touching, and sexually suggestive comments. None of these things are acceptable in the workplace. Yet they are pervasive. And, sometimes, the people enacting such behavior are valuable colleagues. Yes, even "good guys" can behave inappropriately.

"As long as we continue to make it between bad guys and good guys, as long as we keep on doing that, we're never going to get anywhere," New York University psychology professor Niobe Way previously told Quartz.

I know of older men who are seemingly unaware that fawning over a colleague's appearance is inappropriate, and younger, good-looking men who don't seem to realize that yes, their hand resting on a woman's knee or lower back at after-work drinks can be deeply uncomfortable. I don't want these men fired: They can be great mentors and friends. I do want them to stop.

"One size fits all punishment for behavior tends to not do a very good job of getting at the underlying issue," says Davey. "I think many men need to be informed about how they're inadvertently creating discomfort, making women uncomfortable, adding gender politics into the workplace where they don't belong."

Strict, severe punishment could also lead to men being afraid to associate with women—as we've seen in Silicon Valley, where some men have used sexual harassment scandals as an excuse not to have solo meetings or lunches with women. Avoiding women is a form of discrimination in its own right, and hardly innocuous. But even worrying about associating with women could be seriously detrimental to both men and women's careers and workplace relations.

Davey suggests that women respond to smaller instances of inappropriate behavior by calling it out the very first time it happens, letting the colleague know what the offending action was and telling them that it shouldn't be repeated. If it happens again, depending on the severity of the offense, women should feel comfortable giving a stronger admonishment or bringing in a manager or human resources for support. The goal can be to reinforce company policy or educate the perpetrator, rather than immediately firing them. When well-meaning men are inadvertently offensive, making them more self-aware should prevent repeat offenses. Of course, if the behavior doesn't stop, or if it's on the more serious end of the spectrum, then it's absolutely necessary to fire perpetrators.

People who witness inappropriate behavior, rather than directly experiencing it, should also feel confident stepping in. "In many case, the witness to these things is more empowered than the person who is victimized. Especially if power is involved, there's a challenging dynamic for the victim to raise the issue," says Davey. "I strongly encourage people to stop witnessing these things and not saying anything."

The importance of helping men become more self-aware should never be used as an excuse to dismiss concerns about sinister behavior. Sexual harassment can be incredibly insidious and shaped by subtle context. It can involve staring, getting too close, breathing on someone, stroking an arm, licking lips, and all manner of creepy behavior where the malicious intent is only truly obvious to those present.

"Someone's perception is their reality, so hear them out," says Davey. Though it's great if the perpetrator can listen and understand why their behavior made someone uncomfortable, they shouldn't need to understand in order to stop when asked. "They should be motivated to change their behavior to make others comfortable," she adds.

Truly malicious sexual harassers are more common than many would like to believe—and they should be fired. But such perpetrators have been able to get away with their behavior because they act within a cultural environment that treats less severe sexual harassment as tolerable, or even funny. Those who unthinkingly form part of that backdrop—who inadvertently sexual harass without considering why their behavior is harmful—need to be told to change their ways. Only then will the intentional abusers become all the more apparent.

> *"What's fascinating to me is that there are many men who have lived their lives continually throwing grenades and not worrying about how they land."*

# Men Need More Consequences for Bad Behavior

*Sinann Fetherston*

*In the following viewpoint, Sinann Fetherston discusses the #MeToo movement with Deborah Frances-White, who hosts a podcast called The Guilty Feminist. Frances-White says that men often don't know how their actions appear to women. They have never had to understand women or care about their feelings. Men have not had to recognize the consequences of their actions. Powerful men have admitted to harassing women only after they were caught. They then often return to their professional lives quickly. Men convicted of rape have received light sentences. Often, the women accusers suffer more than the men who are accused. That needs to change, this viewpoint says. Raidió Teilifís Éireann is Ireland's national public-service media organisation.*

"Has #MeToo Gone Too Far? The Guilty Feminist Has Her Say," by Sinann Fetherston, Raidió Teilifís Éireann, January 30, 2018. Reprinted by permission.

As you read, consider the following questions:

1. Why do some men not know how to act around women, according to the viewpoint?
2. Why can it be so hard for assault victims to speak up against their accusers?
3. How does power imbalance allow sexual harassment and assault to continue?

One year after #MeToo went viral, we spoke with author and activist Deborah Frances-White aka The Guilty Feminist to discuss why the movement, despite being in its infancy, is being told to back down.

## #MeToo

In 2006, activist Tanara Burke founded the "me too" movement as a way to build a community to help survivors of sexual violence—specifically young women of colour—to recover from their trauma and find pathways of healing.

More than ten years later, on Sunday, October 15th, 2017 actress Alyssa Milano tweeted the words 'me too' and the rest, as they say, is history.

"If you've been sexually harassed or assaulted write 'me too' as a reply to this tweet," she wrote.

The floodgates opened and a tidal wave of women and men shared their experiences of sexual assault, abuse, harassment, and misconduct. What's more, some of those people were famous—as were those they accused.

Viola Davis, Lady Gaga, Reese Witherspoon, America Ferrara, Rose McGowan, Amber Tamblyn, Terry Crews, James Van Der Beek, Gabrielle Union, Ashley Judd and a depressingly long list of survivors shared their stories for all to see.

A month later, the world's press was struggling to keep up with the domino effect of Hollywood's most powerful figures falling into disrepute. Harvey Weinstein, Bill Cosby, Kevin Spacey,

Charlie Rose, Matt Lauer—all accused of varying degrees of sexual misconduct.

The movement has caused controversy, conversation, and change. It has even led to Time's Up, an anti-harassment initiative that calls for equal representation, opportunities, and benefits for minority groups in the LGBTQ community, for women across all industries.

Despite this, some say that #MeToo has gone too far.

## The Guilty Feminist

Australian-born, Britain-based comedian Deborah Frances-White has led a fascinating life. She has moved across continents, spent her teenage years as a Jehovah's Witness, studied English at The University of Oxford, tracked down her birth family, married her podcast producer Tom Salinsky and welcomed Steve Ali, a Syrian refugee, to her home.

Happily, *The Guilty Feminist* podcast spends as much time delving into the host's own life as it does to explore the "noble goals of twenty-first-century feminists and the hypocrisies and insecurities that undermine them".

Now with a book under her belt, we felt it was an opportune moment to speak with the author about the journey of #MeToo and why so many people—men, in particular—are struggling to deal with it.

"What's fascinating to me is that there are many men who have lived their lives continually throwing grenades and not worrying about how they land," Deborah told RTÉ LifeStyle.

"Not knowing whether they're being inappropriately flirtatious, bullying, intimidating, sexually explicit—they just don't know because they've never thought to ask. Even during a sexual experience, they haven't thought to ask. That is fascinating and now there are consequences."

## Empathy and Consequence

During a particular episode of the podcast, called *Taking Control of the Narrative*, Deborah shared her theory as to why some men no longer know how to act around women. For her, it all comes down to empathy.

"I just kind of had a revelation when I heard men say, 'I don't know how to talk to women, I don't feel safe talking to a woman, what if I talk to a woman and she later says I was being lascivious'. I suddenly realised that there are men—it's not all men, it's just some men—that have no idea how they come across to women.

"The men who know how what they say lands, know because they check in with women, either looking for social cues or they ask or they have close female friends who tell them. They are not worried because they know how they come across."

While she has no doubt that these particular men have empathy for their families and even for their colleagues—after all, they would have to understand a manager's feelings and thoughts before asking for a raise—when it came to women, that level of understanding wasn't necessary and so, it simply didn't exist. What's more, there was no consequence.

"Where there was no consequence to their actions, they did not have empathy. And that's how we build empathy in children—we say 'you took that toy from her and now she's crying' and often the child won't have noticed how the other child has reacted so we teach them about consequences by taking the toy away from them and giving it back.

"My hypothesis is that wherever there is a power balance in the world, there is no consequence that has built-in empathy for those abusing the power."

## Forgive and Forget?

On November 9th, 2017, The New York Times reported that five women had stepped forward to accuse comedian Louis C.K. of sexual misconduct. The following day, he responded to the report with a letter that pled guilty to the allegations and ended with him stepping back from the spotlight.

"I have spent my long and lucky career talking and saying anything I want. I will now step back and take a long time to listen. Thank you for reading," he wrote.

By August 2018, Louis. C.K. was back on the stand up circuit.

In a surprise appearance at the Comedy Cellar in New York City, C.K. made no reference to the previous year's allegations in a set that left many audience members feeling ambushed.

While many criticized the stand-up for returning to the stage just months after his departure, others began to question where forgiveness fell into the bigger picture of #MeToo. When was enough, enough? How were these men supposed to make a living?

Comedy Cellar owner Noam Dworman told The New York Times that "there can't be a permanent life sentence on someone who does something wrong."

This was followed up by a tweet from comedian Michael Ian Black who wrote "People have to be allowed to serve their time and move on with their lives. I don't know if it's been long enough, or his career will recover, or if people will have him back, but I'm happy to see him try."

It seems that in less than a year, the anti-sexual harassment movement has been subjected to spectacle, speculation, resistance and now, despite barely finding its feet, an order to cease and desist. Close up shop, it's time to let the men get back to business.

"I would prefer Louis C.K. would do what he said which is to go away and listen for a long time. I don't think under a year is a long time. Under a year is not even a sabbatical," says Frances-White.

"The issue is that he has non-consensually come out and put himself in front of an audience who didn't know they were paying to see him. If Louis C.K. wants to put on a show, then people can decide if they want to see him or not—that's different.

"If you've bought a ticket and you don't know it's going to be him, it's up to you to be the one who walks out and to cause attention and have people maybe tutting at you. And some people may not be able to. They may not have the strength, they may have been victims of this kind of assault and this kind of power abuse and they may not feel comfortable."

She continued: "While it's very good that he admitted it, he wouldn't have admitted it if it wasn't for the Me Too movement. He denied it for years and he gaslighted those women for years and they were sidelined in comedy.

"I don't think it's good enough to say, 'oh, well he said sorry'. He didn't actually use the word sorry, for a start. Secondly, he only confessed when he absolutely had to, not when he could have."

## Whose Future Is Worth More?

Some of the more high profile cases have been treated to speculation due to the time that has passed since the misconduct allegedly happened. Why did the accusers of Bill Cosby, Brett Kavanagh and Harvey Weinstein wait so long to come forward? Frances-White believes the answer lies in the fact that society would rather protect the future of a man over a woman.

On January 18, 2015, two Swedish students were riding their bikes through their college campus when they spotted a man on top of a woman by a dumpster. When they approached them, the man ran away, leaving the unconscious woman alone, and partially naked. That man was later identified as Stanford University swimmer, Brock Turner.

Turner—whose mugshot is now used to illustrate the definition of 'rape' in a criminal justice textbook—faced up to 14 years in state prison when he was convicted of three counts of felony sexual assault.

In the end, he served just three months of his six-month sentence as the judge felt that a longer sentence would have a "severe impact" on the star swimmer.

"For somebody to assault you, they have to have power over you—by definition. Usually, that is physical strength. So, somebody who has power over you has used that power in a way that has hurt you and now you're meant to stand up like David against Goliath and risk getting hurt again," explains Frances-White.

"Why don't they report it? Because somebody who was frightening to them has harmed them and the fear is that they will be further harmed. You're never standing up over somebody over whom you have power and furthermore, the power structures will not believe you and even if they do—like Brock Turner's case where there were independent witnesses—then you'll be told you'll be ruining a young man's future and surely he didn't mean it.

"There is no right time and way to report this kind of abuse but it is always difficult and you need to take that into account."

## Sacrifice

Earlier this year, Dr. Christine Blasey Ford wrote a letter to Rep. Anna Eshoo accusing Brett Kavanaugh (President Donald Trump's Supreme Court nominee) of sexual assault at a party in the 1980's—claims which Kavanaugh heavily denied.

The two were asked to bring their cases before the Senate judiciary committee—the committee tasked with clearing Kavanaugh's nomination prior to the full chamber holding a vote. Ultimately, despite searing testimony from Ford, Judge Brett Kavanaugh was cleared to be sworn in as an Associate Justice of the US Supreme Court by Chief Justice John Roberts.

While many see the result as a loss for the Me Too movement, Frances-White says there is more to be taken from the hearing.

"Dr. Ford. It's a big old sacrifice on her, isn't it? What she has effectively done is re-written the first line of her obituary to include her attacker's name and none of her achievements. That is a huge sacrifice.

"Her name will be linked with his forever and nothing she has ever done or will do will be as lit up as the moment when he allegedly attacked her—so that's a big sacrifice.

"On the face of it, it might seem that she has lost and Me Too lost but the fact that he was even questioned, the fact that he was in the dock in such a high profile way, the fact that it was clearly emotional for him, and the fact that he was not able to take up that position without having to answer serious questions—I think that is its own consequence.

"It's not the consequence we would like, but it is a consequence that is making parent's face their sons and say, 'you must never do this, this may cause consequences now or later in your life.'"

## The Next Generation

Although the possibility of a bad reputation or missed job opportunity shouldn't be the driving force behind the next generation's good behaviour, Frances-White reasons that the result is really all that matters.

"We build consequences for all sorts of things. I don't really care why men aren't attacking women or aren't firing women off their movie sets, I don't care if they need a mercenary motive for it—I care that society empowers and punishes the right thing.

"We need the protection of women to be supported by the power structures. So, even the fact that he had to stand and hear the charges and everybody was looking—will do more to motivate men and motivate parents to tell their sons that there can be a personal cost.

"We need our power structures to support us. It is only right and fair that our power structures support us and just because they haven't done that until now, does not mean they should not do it from here on in."

## A Step Too Far?

So, in one short year, has the movement managed to run away with itself? The Guilty Feminist says it best:

> Whenever I think the Me Too movement has gone too far, I do think the previous "women have to put up with any s\*\*t" movement had a really good run.

> *"The percentage of men who will be afraid to be alone with a female colleague has to be sky high right now."*

# Men Are Afraid of Working with Women

*Erica Alini*

*In the following viewpoint Erica Alini explores potential backlash from the #MeToo movement. Some experts fear that men will avoid being alone with female colleagues because they are afraid of sexual harassment allegations. If they can't be alone with women, they will avoid mentoring women. A poll confirmed that many men avoid working closely with women. This could mean women aren't getting the mentoring and other opportunities that their male coworkers get. In that case, backlash from #MeToo could harm women's careers. On the other hand, some companies are making positive changes in response to #MeToo. They're trying to create a workplace that is fair to all genders.* Global News *is a Canadian media company.*

"'Me Too' Backlash Has Women Worried About Losing Career Opportunities," by Erica Alini, *Global News*, March 9, 2018. Reprinted by permission.

As you read, consider the following questions:

1. How does it harm women if men are afraid of being alone with female coworkers?
2. How has the #MeToo movement encouraged some companies to make changes that could help women?
3. What are other ways that companies could become more fair to women?

The past few months have been quite eventful for women's rights, at least in the Western Hemisphere. It was only October when *The New York Times* published its exposé of now-disgraced Hollywood magnate Harvey Weinstein and the #MeToo hashtag went viral on Twitter. Since then, thousands of women have shared their stories of sexual assault and harassment in the workplace.

All of a sudden, it seemed, the march toward equality had made a huge leap forward.

In the corporate world, there are already warnings that we may be sliding back. Facebook chief operating officer and best-selling *Lean In* author Sheryl Sandberg worried in December that male executives and other men in leadership roles might react to #MeToo by avoiding one-on-one time with female colleagues and underlings out of fear of sexual harassment allegations.

"Four years ago, I wrote in Lean In that 64 per cent of senior male managers were afraid to be alone with a female colleague, in part because of fears of being accused of sexual harassment. The problem with this is that mentoring almost always occurs in one-on-one settings," Sandberg wrote in a long Facebook post.

"The percentage of men who will be afraid to be alone with a female colleague has to be sky high right now," she added.

A month later, a poll conducted by Sandberg's LeanIn.Org foundation and SurveyMonkey confirmed the Facebook executive's worry. Thirty per cent of male managers surveyed said they are uncomfortable working alone with female colleagues, over twice the percentage who said so in the past. Meanwhile, the number of male managers who have concerns about mentoring women more than tripled, from 5 per cent to 16 per cent. All this, despite the fact that nearly half of both men and women said they were not surprised by the recent headlines about sexual harassment and a quarter believe that's only the tip of the iceberg, according to the same survey.

Similar worries are arising in Canada. Lori McIntosh, founder and CEO of Toronto-based Vim and Vixin, which helps place women in executive positions, is increasingly hearing from female clients who worry they will no longer be able to get alone time with their boss to showcase their work.

"I've had this conversation at least four times today already," McIntosh said, speaking to Global News by phone on Tuesday.

## From #MeToo to the Pence Principle

Indeed, McIntosh, whose firms works globally and does most of its business in the U.S. and Canada, says she has experienced the #MeToo backlash herself.

"Some men will not meet alone with me," she said, recalling a recent incident in which she said the CEO of a billion-dollar company specifically alluded to #MeToo after requesting that a third party be present at what was to be a one-on-one meeting.

"It's the first time in 21 years that's happened to me," said McIntosh.

That attitude has also garnered a popular moniker. It's known as the "Pence Principle" or "Pence Rule," in a nod to U.S. Vice-President Mike Pence, who reportedly avoids dining alone or attending events where alcohol is served, without his wife Karen at his side.

"CEOs are very concerned about some of the stories circulating inside their organizations and how to continue to run their business," said McIntosh. But shutting out women is not the answer, she added.

It may not seem like much, but male executives refusing to remain alone with female colleagues could make a big difference because that's when, often, mentoring relationships are formed.

In corporate settings, she says, change tends to come from above. Male leaders need to help women climb the corporate ladder, as they have been for decades with junior male colleagues.

## It's About Men and Women Working Together, Stupid

Male concerns about accusations of sexual harassment in the workplace didn't start with #MeToo, and the movement has prompted a lot of soul-searching at both the individual and corporate levels, said Chi Nguyen, CEO of Toronto-based Parker P Consulting, which helps multinationals, non-governmental organizations and higher education institutions promote gender equality in the workplace.

The onslaught of reports about sexual harassment has many men asking themselves "what is my complacency and what more can I do to stop this from happening," Nguyen said.

Employers, meanwhile, are taking a hard look at their gender equality policies. Here in Canada, the Liberal government's most recent budget hinted that a pay equity law could be coming.

France is also saying "non" to the gender pay gap by asking larger companies to use payroll software to spot and address unexplained differences in compensation between men and women.

That's all well and good, says Nguyen, but policies and rules need to go hand-in-hand with efforts to change the corporate culture.

This isn't about picking the token woman to sit on the corporate board or excluding men from mentoring programs, she says. It's about executives and managers making sure they're searching both gender pools when fishing for top talent.

It's about creating parental leave and flexible schedules and making sure that men are equally expected to take advantage of those workplace perks.

And it's about both men and women trying to understand each other's perspectives and challenges, Nguyen adds.

She recalls the example of a CEO at a resource extraction company who decided to shadow an employee who was a working mom. He noticed the stares she would get from colleagues when leaving at 4 p.m. for "the dinner shift," even though she would come to work at 7 a.m. and often log more hours from the home computer after supper, Nguyen recalled.

But female executives should mentor and shadow their male underlings, too, she added. "It's a two-way street."

#MeToo "is making people stop and think about their behaviours on a daily basis," McIntosh said.

Ultimately, though, "men and women have to work together to make the change."

> *"They were not owed positions of power by virtue of being alive the way we are owed the ability to feel safe in our own skins."*

# Forgiveness Must Be Earned

*Jennifer Wright*

*In the following viewpoint, Jennifer Wright debates whether men should be forgiven for sexual harassment and assault. She finds it hard to be forgiving and even takes pleasure in the downfall of powerful men. Still, she thinks men should be able to make amends and earn forgiveness. She suggests some ways they might do that. Forgiveness is hard, she says, and it shouldn't be given automatically. But in the end, she wants a world where people can be better, and that means believing they can change. Jennifer Wright is a political editor for* Harper's Bazaar.

As you read, consider the following questions:

1. Why does the author suggests that fear might be a good thing for men in power?
2. How can men earn forgiveness for their misdeeds, according to the author?
3. How is justice necessary before forgiveness, according to the viewpoint?

"Should We Forgive Men Accused of Sexual Assault?" by Jennifer Wright, *Harper's Bazaar* a part of Hearst Magazine Media, Inc., March 8, 2018. Reprinted by permission.

Lately, I keep re-reading a certain scene in *Angels in America*. It's a play about gay rights and the incalculable losses of the AIDs years, but it's also a play about America, and morality, and forgiveness.

There is a scene in it where Roy Cohn, a person described as "the polestar of human evil" (and in an interesting note—Donald Trump's old mentor) dies. His nurse asks a friend to say the Kaddish, a prayer of forgiveness, over his body. His friend expresses disbelief that he could be asked to forgive someone who did so much wrong in the world, but, in the end, he does.

It's a beautiful scene. Sometimes, when I think of the long list of men who have done wrongs that have been revealed only lately, I wonder if I could do the same for them. If any of us should forgive them.

It's so difficult.

When I hear a chorus of men saying they are frightened of the times they are living in (frightened of the #MeToo movement), I think of the man who snickered that I could probably get a job at his office if I [performed a sexual act on the boss], or the man who grabbed my a** on the street, or the man who climbed into my bed when I was drunk, or the man who hit me, or the guys who wanted to drive really slowly next to me as I walked home late at night, and I think: "F*** their fear. We've been scared plenty. What we are taking from them is nothing compared to what they've taken from us."

Men have had so much privilege for so long. It certainly feels that white men have never had to suffer much in the way of consequences.

So, I see men fall from grace and I rejoice, because I do not think you are owed an extremely well paying job if you behave like a scumbag to the people who have to work with you. I do not think that getting fired and taking a large buy-out package is "the ultimate degradation."

They were not owed positions of power by virtue of being alive the way we are owed the ability to feel safe in our own skins.

They think they've suffered? Please.

Watching this feels good. More than that, it feels righteous. It is hard for me, I think for many of us (at least, I hope it's not just me) to feel like sympathizing, let alone forgiving.

I told my conservative mother (who was a corporate VP in the '80s) that I was thinking of writing on the topic of how women could begin to forgive, and she paused for a long moment and said, "Do you think you could wait until a few more men in business get taken down, first?"

Maybe their being afraid isn't such a bad thing.

Maybe some fear will make men more thoughtful about their actions. Maybe it will make some of the men growing up now, in an age of consequences, require less forgiveness in the future.

But what of the men of the current age? There is a long list of the ones who have done wrong and been outed for it, and there are many more who should be scared. There are men who have done bad things to women, and we sometimes find ourselves in the terrible position of loving (or at least liking) those men who have done those bad things.

It may be that they are artists whose work we have enjoyed. More difficult, it may be that they are friends, or our husbands or brothers. There are a great many men we would not want to write off entirely.

So what can be done in those cases?

I believe that they should make reparation for their misdeeds. But I believe there must be a path to redemption, too. While we think about men who must be removed from their positions of power, we should also think about what those men can do to earn redemption in our eyes. We should be asking that, insofar as forgiveness is possible, what would merit it?

Off the top of my head, as far as notable men go, I'd like to see them work behind the scenes to facilitate female creators, donate to organizations like Time's Up, fight for pay equality, stop hedging their apologies (because these public conflicts ultimately have to be healed the same way private conflicts are healed, with genuine acknowledgement of wrongdoing), and accepting that their careers might be over instead of fighting tooth and nail to remain in the public eye, and, possibly, serving a prison term.

I have very little interest in forgiving people who seem uninterested in apologizing for any misdeeds (Bill Cosby, Woody Allen, Donald Trump, who continue to deny allegations of sexual abuse). Frankly, f*** those guys.

But I think there are also men who are interested in doing better, who do feel genuine guilt and sorrow for the wrongs they've done, and would like to be better in the future.

Because I am a progressive, I believe people can progress. I don't want the men whose bad deeds have been exposed by the #MeToo movement to be sent off to an island forever. I want them to learn, and choose to be better people.

There is a lot to be said for cleaning away the awfulness of old values, where we accepted that men could do whatever they wanted, and that was just the way it was. But after we tear down the world, we will need to rebuild it.

I hope we will build a world where we have faith that humans can be better. Even if it's naïve, even if it's often disproved. That is the nature of hope and faith. And I hope we can extend that sometimes foolish optimism even to humans who have done bad things, and treat humans in a way where they need not be reduced to the bad things they have done. We can, each of us, change, and strive towards what is good.

Because what is there, really, beyond hope that people can be better? Women have rarely been in a position to be angry before, but we've rarely been in a position where our forgiveness was not automatically assumed before. Giving it out judiciously to those who earn it, that too, is a kind of power we deserve.

It will not be easy, I do not think. At least not for me. But as *Angels in America* says:

> It isn't easy. It doesn't count if it's easy. It's the hardest thing. Forgiveness. Which is maybe where love, and justice finally meet.

> *"It is almost like Cavill wants us all to know who the real victims of #MeToo are. It's decent men like him, who just want to be able to 'flirt' but who are surrounded by malevolent, deceitful, lying women who are just waiting for a flirty smile from Mr. Cavill so he can be whisked off to prison."*

# #MeToo Is Not a "Witchhunt," and Men Are Not Its Victims

*Taryn De Vere*

*In the following viewpoint Taryn De Vere exposes the absurdity in men portraying themselves as victims in the #MeToo movement. The author focuses on reactions from men in show business who have publicly expressed nonchalance over accusations aimed at their male colleagues as well as fear of being accused themselves. De Vere argues that these men have failed to understand who the real victims are, and in fact may be missing the point of the #MeToo movement altogether. The fact that #MeToo has been labelled a witchhunt shows that there is still much progress to be made in the fight for women's equality. Taryn De Vere is a writer and parenting coach.*

"The Real Victims of #MeToo? Men," by Taryn De Vere, Medium.com, July 13, 2018. Reprinted by permission.

As you read, consider the following questions:

1. According to the viewpoint, what is missing from the interactions Liam Neeson and Terry Gilliam seem to view as harmless?
2. How has actor Henry Cavill missed the point of #MeToo, according to the author?
3. How does the author bring up her personal experience in this viewpoint?

Imagine for a minute, that women who work in the same industry as you begin to speak openly about the sexual harassment, rape and abuse they have experienced. Then women from other industries begin to speak out about what happened to them until eventually, in an unprecedented outpouring of horror—millions of women all around the world also share their stories of sexual assault.

How do you respond?

Liam Neeson suggested that the outing of the perpetrators responsible amounted to a "witchhunt."

As if men being held accountable for abusing their power over women by sexually assaulting them was comparable with women being burnt alive for being too clever or outspoken.

Neeson also said of the sexual harassment Dustin Hoffman was accused of, "When you're doing a play and you're with your family (other actors, technicians) you do silly things…and it becomes kind of superstitious, if you don't do it every night you think it's going to jinx the show."

Multiple women have accused Hoffman of sexual assault, including women who were underage at the time of the alleged assaults. "Silly things" are all well and good, provided they are consensual, however the idea that repeated sexual assault was essential to the success of a theatre show is sinister in the extreme.

Director Terry Gilliam said the #MeToo movement had created a "world of victims."

Gilliam didn't seem to be saying this in a "I'm-so-shocked-millions-of-women-have-experienced-sexual-assault" kind of way. His comments had more the flavour of "stop your whining" about them, but perhaps I am being ungenerous.

Speaking about Harvey Weinstein who has been accused of numerous sexual assaults Gilliam said, "Harvey opened the door for a few people, a night with Harvey—that's the price you pay."

"I think some people did very well out of meeting with Harvey and others didn't. The ones who did, knew what they were doing. These are adults; we are talking about adults with a lot of ambition."

Gilliam makes it sound as if every woman who has accused Weinstein was fully aware that sex was expected of them, and consented to it in order to progress their career. This is despite the testimony of the women themselves, which tells a very different story. But, ambition right?

This week bought Justice League actor, Henry Cavill and his "take" on #MeToo. In an interview with GQ Australia, Cavill was asked for his thoughts on the #MeToo movement, "It's very difficult to do that if there are certain rules in place. Because then it's like: 'Well, I don't want to go up and talk to her, because I'm going to be called a rapist or something.'"

"I'm someone in the public eye, and if I go and flirt with someone, then who knows what's going to happen?" he said. "Now? Now you really can't pursue someone further than, 'No'. It's like, 'OK, cool'. But then there's the 'Oh why'd you give up?' and it's like 'Well, because I didn't want to go to jail?'"

It is almost like Cavill wants us all to know who the real victims of #MeToo are. It's decent men like him, who just want to be able to "flirt" but who are surrounded by malevolent, deceitful, lying women who are just waiting for a flirty smile from Mr Cavill so he can be whisked off to prison.

Perhaps Cavill is unaware that of every 1000 rapes 994 perpetrators will walk free. Perhaps he does not know how few women even report the crimes against them, and how hard it is to secure a conviction.

# #MeToo Has Become Unrecognizable

The founder of the #MeToo movement has said the campaign she started against sexual violence has become unrecognisable and misrepresented as a vindictive plot against men.

Tarana Burke, an American civil rights activist, started the campaign in 2006 with the goal of providing support to survivors of sexual violence in her community. Last year the phrase took off globally in the wake of allegations against the Hollywood mogul Harvey Weinstein.

Burke told a TEDWomen event in Palm Springs, California, that parts of the media had framed the movement as a witch-hunt and that US politicians seemed to be "pivoting away from the issue" in the wake of events such as the controversy over Brett Kavanaugh's appointment to the supreme court.

"Suddenly, a movement to centre survivors of sexual violence is being talked about as a vindictive plot against men," she told the audience. "This is a movement about the one in four girls and the one in six boys who are sexually abused every year, and who carry those wounds into adulthood," she said. "Victims are heard and then vilified."

Burke said she wanted the movement to return to the issues she set out to challenge over a decade ago.

"My vision for the #MeToo movement is part of a collective vision to see a world free of sexual violence," she said. "I believe we can build that world. Full stop."

"We owe future generations nothing less than a world free of sexual violence. This accumulation of feelings that so many of us are feeling together across the globe is collective trauma."

Burke said she felt the campaign was neglecting victims of sexual violence, adding: "This movement has been called a watershed moment, but some days I wake up feeling that all the evidence points to the contrary.

"We have to re-educate ourselves and our children to understand that power and privilege doesn't always have to destroy and take. It can be used to serve and build."

"#MeToo Has Been Misrepresented as Plot Against Men, Says Founder", by Patrick Greenfield, Guardian News and Media Limited, November 30, 2018.

"There's something wonderful about a man chasing a woman. There's a traditional approach to that, which is nice, I think a woman should be wooed and chased, but maybe I'm old-fashioned for thinking that."

"Now you really can't pursue someone further than, 'No.'" says Cavill.

I would like to ask Mr Cavill who men chasing women is wonderful for? I can only speak for myself but I do not like the idea of being "chased", like I am some kind of prey to be hunted down. Cavill seems to view women as conquests to be caught, secured and "wooed". Perhaps there are women who like that, however most women (I think) just want to be treated as autonomous human beings, whose "No" will be respected.

But don't worry lads, we get it. The current climate of not being able to press a woman after she says "No" has been tough for some of you. When women call for some accountability and consequences for rapists and abusers it's a "witchhunt" against the real victims—men.

For poor Mr Cavill it has meant he has had to call up his ex-girlfriends instead, "and just go back to a relationship, which never really worked." He says he has to do this because, "it's way safer than casting myself into the fires of hell."

As a rape victim I know about the "fires of hell." The hell of knowing I would not be believed. The hell of having my body used and abused against my will. The hell of knowing I would never see any justice for the crimes committed against me. But what is the pain of a rape victim when compared to a rich, privileged, white, male celebrity as he worries about if his "wooing" technique could be construed as sexual assault?

If Mr Cavill doesn't know how to communicate his interest in a women in a way that doesn't feel like sexual assault, then maybe it's best he does stay away from women.

# Periodical and Internet Sources Bibliography

*The following articles have been selected to supplement the diverse views presented in this chapter.*

"After a Year of #MeToo, American Opinion Has Shifted Against Victims." The *Economist*. Oct. 15th 2018. https://www.economist.com/graphic-detail/2018/10/15/after-a-year-of-metoo-american-opinion-has-shifted-against-victims.

John Baldoni, "Shame Them: One Way to Hold Men Accountable for Sexual Abuse," Forbes, Nov. 16, 2017. https://www.forbes.com/sites/johnbaldoni/2017/11/16/shame-them-one-way-to-holding-men-accountable-for-sexual-abuse/#1c7da52e3c5a.

Caterina Bulgarella, "What Happens When Women Stop Protecting Men: Understanding the #MeToo's Backlash," Forbes, Oct. 18, 2018. https://www.forbes.com/sites/caterinabulgarella/2018/10/18/what-happens-when-women-stop-protecting-men-understanding-the-metoos-backlash/#5c8f81ac2088.

Susan G. Cole, "Backlash to Aziz Ansari Story Shows Why #MeToo Hasn't Gone Far Enough," Now Toronto, Jan. 18, 2018. https://nowtoronto.com/news/aziz-ansari-backlash-shows-metoo-hasnt-gone-far-enough/.

Larry Kummer, "Worrying While the Harassment Fires Burn Out of Control," Fabius Maximus, Dec. 6, 2017. https://fabiusmaximus.com/2017/12/06/sexual-harassment-reconsidered/.

Olivia Lewke, "Why the #MeToo Movement Is Not About Women Overreacting in the Workplace," *Caliber* magazine, Mar. 4, 2018. https://www.calibermag.net/blog/2018/3/4/why-the-metoo-movement-is-not-about-women-overreacting-in-the-workplace.

David Roberts, "What So Many Men Are Missing about #MeToo," Vox, Sep. 12, 2018. https://www.vox.com/2018/9/10/17826168/me-too-louis-ck-men-comeback.

Pooja Singh, "How the #MeToo Movement Is Affecting Men at the Workplace," Entrepreneur, Dec. 5, 2018. https://www.entrepreneur.com/article/324331.

Tovia Smith, "On #MeToo, Americans More Divided by Party Than Gender," NPR, Oct. 31, 2018. https://www.npr.

org/2018/10/31/662178315/on-metoo-americans-more-divided-by-party-than-gender.

Debra Soh, "Do the Men of #MeToo Deserve to Be Forgiven?" *Globe and Mail*, Sep. 6, 2018. https://www.theglobeandmail.com/opinion/article-do-the-men-of-metoo-deserve-to-be-forgiven/.

Katherine Tarbox, "Is #MeToo Backlash Hurting Women's Opportunities in Finance?" *Harvard Business Review*, Mar. 12, 2018. https://hbr.org/2018/03/is-metoo-backlash-hurting-womens-opportunities-in-finance.

OPPOSING
VIEWPOINTS®
SERIES

CHAPTER 3

# Whom Should We Believe?

# Chapter Preface

It's easy to make accusations. It can be much harder to prove them. Sexual harassment and assault often take place in private, with no witnesses. The victim may describe the situation one way. The accused may claim something entirely different happened. Who should be believed?

It's hard to determine exactly how many accusations are false. A tiny percentage is eventually proven to be false, but nobody knows the real numbers for sure. Most sources agree that false accusations of rape or sexual assault are very rare. On the other hand, statistics show that most victims never come forward, so most offenders are never punished. Even when cases go to court, and the accused are found guilty, many get off with light sentences or probation.

Still, a false accusation can destroy someone's career. Students have been expelled from college. Men have lost jobs. A few have gone to jail for crimes they didn't commit. How do we balance "believe women" when they say they have been assaulted, with "innocent until proven guilty" under the law?

One viewpoint author in this chapter points out that the media has a good record of carefully investigating claims. "Believe women" does not mean skipping rigorous journalism. Nor does it mean skipping fair treatment through the legal system, known as due process. Another viewpoint notes that believing women is a way of supporting a healthy legal system. Too often, courts have humiliated and demonized the victims. They have relied on stereotypes about "loose women" who "ask for it." They assume that someone who can't remember details, or whose story changes, is lying. In reality, victims of assault often have confused memories due to trauma. By understanding the realities of assault, the law could better protect victims and punish criminals.

Yet another viewpoint asks people to tread cautiously. Wait until all the facts come to light before deciding whether to believe a claim. It's not fair to destroy a person's reputation without proof. On the other hand, one author says that harming a person's reputation is not the same as legal punishment. A damaged reputation may hurt, but it's not equal to being the victim of assault. Therefore, it's more important to protect the victims of assault than to protect the few victims of false accusations. In any case, someone who is wrongly accused can use the law to sue their accuser for defamation.

Finally, one viewpoint notes that sexual harassment and assault aren't really about sex or gender. They're about the abuse of power. As such, it's not enough to try individual cases, either in the law courts or in the court of public opinion. Instead, society needs to change. To do this, we should focus on changing the imbalance of power, instead of arguing about whom to believe.

> *"However, what about those men who are stand up guys and their reputation impeccable and they are falsely accused of a sexual assault?"*

# Wait for the Facts

*Professor Ron*

*In the following viewpoint, "Professor Ron" cautions against a broad practice of believing all victims before understanding the details of each situation. The author expresses concern for men who are falsely accused of sexual assault. He notes that, although false accusations are rare, they can greatly harm someone's reputation—sometimes irrevocably. Even when the law determines that a person is innocent, they have suffered humiliation. In some cases, students have been expelled from college due to claims later shown to be false. The author advises waiting until all the facts come to light before making a decision about whether to believe a claim. Professor Ron is an associate professor of sociology.*

As you read, consider the following questions:

1. How can a false accusation harm someone, according to the author?
2. Why do people want to believe false claims, according to the author?
3. What should people do when a sexual assault allegation is made, according to the author?

## Hale to the Chief?

"It is true rape is a most detestable crime, and therefore ought severely and impartially to be punished with death; but it must be remembered, that it is an accusation easily to be made and hard to be proved, and harder to be defended by the party accused, tho never so innocent"

(Hale, 1847, pg. 634).

This quote by Sir Matthew Hale, who was an influential English barrister, judge and lawyer in the 1600's is unequivocally one of the truest statements in history regarding rape. I understand that some people may disagree with Hale's perspective regarding the latter aspects of his quote, however, it can't be argued that a person falsely accused of (any) crime (rape, murder, arson, shoplifting, etc.), shouldn't be made a pariah prior to due process being given to said person.

## Hey, Don't Forget #MeToo!

The #MeToo movement has raised the awareness of a nation, making way for women to voice how difficult it is for them to move through society without being harassed, sexually assaulted, and intimidated and/or abused (Dastagir, 2017). Moreover, this movement has forced prominent politicians out of office (i.e. Sen. Al Franken, Rep. Trent Franks) over sexual misconduct allegations, while at the same time depicting these same men as monsters and pariahs, unfit to hold office due to their past transgressions. In the same vein, and perhaps most notably, Hollywood moguls such as Harvey Weinstein have been brought down to size based on claims of sexual improprieties and inappropriate behavior toward women. In these examples, perhaps it's justified to expect their resignations from their respective posts due to their own admissions to wrong doing or the abundance of evidence that suggest (or proves their guilt). However, what about those men who are stand up guys and their reputation impeccable and they are falsely accused of a sexual assault?

## Labeling Theory, Stigmatization and Societal Reaction

Let me be clear, any individual (male or female) who forces another person into doing something against their will, especially in regards to sexual assault should be labeled deviant and dealt with according to the law. However, there will and has been situations in which individuals, mostly men, have been falsely accused of a sexual assault. Unfortunately, the time is upon us where these men are not getting the due process they deserve according to the law, while simultaneously their reputations are being called into question by the community and society as a whole.

Ultimately, all a person has in the end is their reputation and what they represent. Therefore, labeling individuals as a sexual assaulter is a serious moniker and needs to be carefully applied. Unfortunately, in certain situations, this expectation is not adhered to, thus allowing for the accused to become a pariah, an outsider. Howard Becker (1963) explains it best regarding how an individual is tagged with a particular label:

> …social groups create deviance by making the rules whose infraction constitutes deviance, and by applying those rules to particular people and labeling them as outsiders. From this point of view, deviance is not a quality of the act the person commits, but rather a consequence of the application by others of rules and sanctions to an "offender". The deviant is one to

## The Risks of "Believing Women"

The costly toll of "believing women," instead of believing evidence, can be seen in the hundreds and hundreds of cases recorded by the University of Michigan Law School's National Registry of Exonerations involving innocent men falsely accused of rape and rape/murders.

One of those men whose plight I've reported on for CRTV and my syndicated column, former Fort Worth police officer Brian Franklin, spent 21 years of a life sentence in prison after he was convicted in 1995 of sexually assaulting a 13-year-old girl who had committed perjury on the stand. Franklin vigilantly maintained his innocence, studied law in the prison library, and won a reversal of his conviction in 2016. The jury took less than two hours to acquit him.

The idea that all women and girls must be telling the truth at all times about sexual-assault allegations because they "have nothing to gain" is perilously detached from reality. Retired NYPD special-victims-squad detective John Savino, forensic scientist and criminal profiler of the Forensic Criminology Institute Brent Turvey, and forensic psychologist Aurelio Coronado Mares detail the myriad "prosocial" and "antisocial" lies people tell in their textbook *False Allegations: Investigative and Forensic Issues in Fraudulent Reports of Crime*.

who that label has successfully been applied; deviant behavior is behavior that people so label

Arguably, the #MeToo movement is essentially a (social group's) created standard. A standard from the stand point that even an accusation of sexual impropriety, particularly towards a woman, counts as an infraction against the new rules of social consciousness regarding sexual assault victims. The accused now carries the label of being a deviant, which has been successfully applied to them.

Of course there are those who will scoff at this perspective and note that the percentage of false allegations of sexual assault are rare. In fact, Lisak, Gardinier, Nicksa, and Cote (2010) found in their study that over a 10-year period the prevalence of false

"Prosocial deceptions" involve specific motives beneficial to both the deceiver and the deceived, including the incentives to "preserve the dignity of others"; to gain "financial benefit" for another; to protect a relationship; for "ego-boosting or image protection (of others)"; and for "protecting others from harm or consequence."

"Antisocial" lies involve selfish motives to "further a personal agenda at some cost to others," including "self-deception and rationalization to protect or boost self-esteem"; "enhance status or perception in the eyes of others"; "garner sympathy"; "avoid social stigma"; "conceal inadequacy, error, and culpability"; "avoid consequence"; and for "personal and/or material gain."

Let me repeat the themes of my work in this area for the past two years to counter the "Believe Women" baloney:

The role of the press should be verification, not validation.

Rape is a devastating crime. So is lying about it.

It's not victim-blaming to get to the bottom of the truth. It's liar-shaming.

Don't believe a gender. Believe evidence.

**"Don't 'Believe Women.' Believe Evidence," by Michelle Malkin, *National Review*, September 19, 2018.**

allegations of sexual assault ranged between 2% and 10%. It is my contention that even though false allegations of sexual assault are rare, the small percentage of individuals who are falsely accused are still having the label of a deviant applied to them. According to Goffman (1963) people who become associated with a stigmatized situation pass from a "normal" to a "discredited" or "discreditable" social status. Furthermore, Kleinman and Hall-Clifford (2009) suggest that stigma decays one's ability to hold on to what matters most to people in a local world, such as wealth, relationships, and life chances. It is important to remember that the stigmatized and those who stigmatize are interconnected through local social networks (Kleinman and Hall-Clifford, 2009, pg. 3).

## Social Media and Public Opinion

In 2006, activist Tarana Burke started what has now famously become the #MeToo movement. However, the hashtag that represents the social cause can be attributed to the actress Alyssa Milano. Milano used the hashtag in an effort to support her friend Rose McGowan who made allegations of sexual harassment against the now disgraced Harvey Weinstein.

However, there is an argument to be made that there is already pushback growing against the #MeToo movement. According to Weiss (2017), there will come a time where there will be a false accusation in the likes of the Duke Lacrosse moment, or the University of Virginia moment in which a purported group sexual assault took place on campus, and *Rolling Stone* ended up writing, a now retracted article, *A Rape on Campus*, which turned out to fabricated.

Unfortunately, the truth tends to get lost in the minutiae of social media. The court of public opinion often has the tendency to disregard facts and cling to salaciousness as a newborn to their mother's breast. One case in point is that of college students Catherine Reddington and Alex Goldman. This is a classic case of a young woman in a frat house drunk off her rocker and wakes up in the bed with a man and doesn't know what happened the night before, but claims she was raped. However, according to police reports, the two both woke up fully clothed in Goldman's bed the next morning after the alleged incident. What's more, the investigation into Reddington's claims went on for several months, which included a medical exam, rape kit and bloodwork within 26 hours of the incident and found no evidence that Reddington had been assaulted, drugged or even had sex with Goldman. (Boniello, 2018). In addition, the assistant district attorney said this about why Goldman was never charged:

> "Investigators found it "impossible to determine what, if anything, occurred that evening between Ms. Reddington and Mr. Goldman. There is no credible (proof) of any sexual conduct in this case, consensual or non-consensual" (Boniello, 2018).

Yet and still, with all these facts in the foreground, Ms. Reddington took to Facebook in attempt to plead her case, or in perhaps what Mr. Goldman would believe, to smear his name, even though he was never charged with a sexual assault crime. To add insult to injury, Ms. Reddington's false accusations got Goldman kicked out of Syracuse University. It is also believed that Reddington's social-media posts are targeting Goldman's new school and employer in an attempt to further tarnish his reputation. What is concerning about this particular situation is that not only is an innocent man tormented by false allegations, but that people on social-media, specifically commenting on Reddington's synopsis about what transpired the night she was supposedly "raped" and "sodomized" are cheering her (Reddington) on as some sort of hero. Just scroll down to the comments and you will see replies such as, "you are so strong, keep being beautiful," "So brave. You are so strong," "We're with you all the way." These types of responses are quite delusional given the facts of the case. How is she (Reddington) so brave and strong? Why are people with her "all the way" when the law has admitted that Mr. Goldman is innocent from any wrong doing? The reason in my estimation is because social media loves to tear down and destroy anyone in its path, regardless of the facts.

## Nikki Yovino Case

Take the case of the two college football players from Sacred Heart University, Malik St. Hilaire and (unnamed). These two young men were initially charged with raping Nikki Yovino in a bathroom during an off-campus party. Detectives believed her at first and had witness statements that seemed to corroborate her story, and it appeared the investigation was leading to charging the two students. However, months later she admitted to police her allegations were all a ruse to garner sympathy from a prospective boyfriend. More specifically, it turns out Yovino didn't want this prospective boyfriend to view her as (promiscuous) so in turn, she claimed her sexual, consensual, encounter with the two football players was a forced event (Rhett-Miller, 2017).

Although Yovino later admitted that her allegations were all a lie, the spoiled identity of the two young men had already been done. Mr. Hilaire gave a victim impact statement at sentencing confronting Yovino:

> "I went from being a college student to sitting at home being expelled, with no way to clear my name," St. Hilaire told the judge, as Yovino smirked just a few feet away. "I just hope she knows what she has done to me. My life will never be the same. I did nothing wrong, but everything has been altered because of this."

## In a Perfect World

There are plenty of men in the world who are loving and kind. It's very disappointing to see masculinity under attack by so many in society. Moreover, it's sad to have the entire male species labelled as barbarians. *In a perfect world*, when a sexual assault allegation is made, withholding judgment until all the facts have had an opportunity to manifest would be best. Instead of following the faux outrage of social media and mainstream media corporations, individuals should practice reservation and restraint. Perhaps this idea is a pipe dream that will never come to fruition, but one can still hope.

## References

Becker, H. S. (1963). Outsiders; studies in the sociology of deviance. London: Free Press of Glencoe.

Boniello, K. (2018, June, 30). False college rape allegation "destroyed" my life: suit. New York Post. Retrieved from https://nypost.com/2018/06/30/false-college-rape-allegation-destroyed-my-life-suit/

Borge, J. (2018, January, 7). Who Started the Me Too Movement? Retrieved from https://www.instyle.com/news/who-started-me-too-movement

Goffman, E. (1963). Stigma: Notes on the Management of Spoiled Identity. New York: Prentice-Hall.

Hale, M., In Stokes, W. A., In Ingersoll, E., & Emlyn, S. (1847). Historia placitorum coronae: The history of the pleas of the crown. Philadelphia: R.H. Small.

Harvey Weinstein scandal: Who has accused him of what? (2018, May, 25), BBC. Retrieved from https://www.bbc.com/news/entertainment-arts-41580010

Kleinman, Arthur and Rachel Hall-Clifford. Forthcoming. (2009). Stigma: A social, cultural, and moral process. Journal of Epidemiology and Community Health 63(6).

Lisak, D., Gardinier, L., Nicksa, S. C., & Cote, A. M. (2010). False allegations of sexual assault: An analysis of ten years of reported cases. Violence Against Women, 16(12), 1318–1334.

Marie, Catherine. (June 4). In Facebook. Retrieved (September, 26, 2018). https://www.facebook.com/kay.tee.585/posts/10215868923373744

Miller, R.J. (2017, February, 22). Teen Charged with lying about being raped by college football players. New York Post. Retrieved from https://nypost.com/2017/02/22/teen-charged-with-lying-about-being-raped-by-college-football-players/

Richer, D.A. (2017, June, 13). Rolling Stone to pay $1.65 to settle suit over rape story. Associated Press. Retrieved from https://apnews.com/d78870b25d2d4cd8b06c99ae34001406

Some say one false report could cripple the #MeToo movement. Is progress that fragile? (2017, December, 8), USA Today. Retrieved from https://www.usatoday.com/story/news/2017/12/08/analysis-movement-metoo-but-heres-why-were-still-talking-believewomen/923156001/

Weiss, B. (2017, November, 28). "The Limits of "Believe All Women". New York Times. Retrieved from https://www.nytimes.com/2017/11/28/opinion/metoo-sexual-harassment-believe-women.html

> "*#MeToo is about fixing the system, once and for all—a system that treats accusers as liars, subjects them to brutal questioning, and damages their reputation.*"

# Believe Women for a Better Legal System

*Don Lenihan*

*In the following viewpoint, Don Lenihan delves further into the idea of believing women. Does automatically believing women go against the philosophy of innocent until proven guilty? In this author's view, believing women may actually lead to a better and fairer legal system. It would mean trusting women equally to men, rather than using stereotypes to discredit victims. It would mean developing a better understanding of how assault victims remember events and behave afterward. It would mean not destroying the lives of the accusers in order to protect the accused. Don Lenihan writes for National Newswatch, a Canadian political news site.*

As you read, consider the following questions:

1. How can "believe the accuser" mean getting rid of stereotypes?
2. Why can a victim's poor memory of events around an assault support the idea that the assault happened?
3. Why are some people skeptical of evidence supported by social science, according to the author?

#MeToo may be powered by outrage, but it is a purposeful outrage. The women coming forward and standing together know what they want to change and why. Take Canada: between 2009 and 2014, only one in 10 sexual assault charges resulted in a conviction. And the other 90 per cent? Well, either the accusers were liars, or the justice system failed—catastrophically.

#MeToo is about fixing the system, once and for all—a system that treats accusers as liars, subjects them to brutal questioning, and damages their reputation. An acceptable alternative, as the movement says, must start by believing the accusers.

But what does that mean? Lots of people are confused about this. Do we dispense with due process? Are we setting aside the presumption of innocence? People want to know how a better system will work.

Canadians are especially sensitive to the dilemma. We watched our prime minister impale himself on it. As a progressive and feminist, Justin Trudeau declared his willingness to believe the accusers—to the point of rapidly expelling two caucus members for alleged improprieties, only to find himself ensnared in similar charges from his youth.

But if failed experiments like this one make us cautious about a more "progressive" approach, recent debates, like the one now raging over Ford/Kavanaugh, are more heartening. Generally, experts are not calling on the courts to abandon due process, so much as to double down on it. They want better and more rigorous standards, not weaker ones.

Take consent. Too often it comes down to stereotyping. For example, the "loose woman" might include wearing short skirts, frequenting bars, and flirting with men. If a profile of an accuser can be made to match these criteria, the stereotype is taken as evidence of her character and intentions.

This kind of reasoning has a long history in the jurisprudence and far too many cases still turn on it. But stereotyping has been widely discredited, and not just for sexual assault. Human behavior turns out to be indelibly complex. Divining someone's character and intentions from a template (stereotype) is not only simplistic, it is offensive.

So, to "believe the accuser" here doesn't mean suspending due process. It means getting rid of stereotyping. It calls on the courts to raise their standard of proof. Consent should be a process in which both partners play an active role and have mutual responsibilities. Specifically, before initiating sex, an actor should seek verbal agreement—and in such an exchange, no always means no.

What about the presumption of innocence?

Suppose a woman accuses a man of sexual harassment or assault. Often, there will be no other witnesses, so their testimony will be the principal source of evidence. If their stories disagree, as they likely will, they are usually assumed to cancel one another out—the proverbial "he said/she said." The accused is therefore presumed innocent.

That's how Clarence Thomas maneuvered around Anita Hill in 1991. It is how Brett Kavanaugh will hope to prevail over Christine Blasey Ford this week. However, recent research sheds new light on such a defense. It shows how circumstances traditionally thought to discredit an accuser's testimony can in fact support it.

For example, a sketchy memory of the events around an assault normally casts doubt on the accuser's testimony. Phenomena like this could form part of an overall psychological profile of victims of sexual assault—much like victims of other psychological traumas.

In this context, a sketchy memory might provide support for an accuser's story, rather than undermining it. Creating such a profile may not be easy, but there is encouraging evidence that it can be done.

The point is that the more we learn about sexual assault, the more it changes how we view what counts as evidence. By-and-large, this is lending accusers' testimony a new kind of credibility that can offset the he said/she said problem.

In an op-ed in the *New York Times* last week, Anita Hill underlines the critical role that a rigorous process and reliable research can play in breaking this deadlock. She calls on the Senate committee investigating the Ford/Kavanaugh case to:

> …demonstrate a clear understanding that sexual violence is a social reality to which elected representatives must respond. A fair, neutral and well-thought-out course is the only way to approach Dr. Blasey and Judge Kavanaugh's forthcoming testimony. The details of what that process would look like should be guided by experts who have devoted their careers to understanding sexual violence…the weight of the government should not be used to destroy the lives of witnesses who are called to testify.

Nevertheless, many Republicans, specifically, and conservatives, generally, fiercely resist the introduction of this kind of evidence and expertise into the courts. It is the thin edge of a much bigger wedge. They see social science—and especially sociology—as the bible of liberal judges, who will use it to justify all manner of "judge-made law." And that drives them to distraction.

But what is the alternative? Without this kind of learning, conventional wisdom and discredited practices will continue to dominate the system.

And we will be left struggling to explain why so many cases fail to result in a conviction. Does anyone really believe these accusers are all liars?

> *"Those concerned about the failure of a legal principle in relation to #MeToo might better focus on that of justice for victims."*

# Worry About Victims, Not Loss of Reputation for Accusers

*Cristy Clark*

*In the following viewpoint, Cristy Clark argues that critics say #MeToo goes against the principle of a fair trial and "innocent until proven guilty." "Trial by Twitter," judging someone guilty through social media, may harm that person's reputation. However, she states, that is not comparable to legal punishment. Social media accusations give a voice to the victim, who may suffer unfairly from trying to get legal support. If a person is wrongly accused, they could sue. If someone makes a false statement that causes injury or damage, that is defamation, which is illegal. Forms of defamation include libel, which is made in writing, and slander, which is spoken. Cristy Clark teaches human rights and competition and consumer law at the Southern Cross University School of Law and Justice in Australia.*

As you read, consider the following questions:

1. What does "trial by Twitter" really imply, according to the author?
2. Why are victims turning to social media to accuse their harassers, according to the article?
3. How does the #MeToo movement help protect the rights of victims, according to the author?

C ritics have raised concerns that #MeToo has turned into a "trial by Twitter," suggesting it has turned the legal principle of innocent until proven guilty on its head. The Australian's opinion columnist Janet Albrechtsen argued this point on the ABC's #MeToo Q&A special last month.

But such comments reveal an ignorance of the meaning and context of this principle. Leaving aside the fact that some people on social media side with the accused, public discussion—whether it takes place on Twitter or around a water cooler—is not comparable to state punishment.

Those concerned about the failure of a legal principle in relation to #MeToo might better focus on that of justice for victims.

## The Right to an Untarnished Reputation

Broadly speaking, there are three core elements to #MeToo.

First, the sheer volume of disclosures highlights that sexual harassment and abuse are unacceptably widespread—and that institutions and society at large are failing to protect and support victims. Then there is the practice of using the hashtag to challenge the stigma and shame that has somehow accompanied identifying as a victim. Finally, some disclosures on Twitter have sought to name and shame perpetrators of abuse in order to seek accountability and justice.

Only this third element plausibly raises concerns around "trial by Twitter." So, before delving into the problematic subtext of these comments, I'm going to play devil's advocate and consider whether these public accusations do conflict with the presumption of innocence.

The presumption of innocence is enshrined in Article 14.2 of the International Covenant on Civil and Political Rights. It states simply that,

> Everyone charged with a criminal offence shall have the right to be presumed innocent until proved guilty according to law.

A related right, enshrined in Articles 14.1 and 14.3, is the right to a fair trial, which includes equality before the law and,

> a fair and public hearing by a competent, independent and impartial tribunal established by law.

In relation to the public accusations levelled on #MeToo, this means that if someone is charged with a criminal offence, the system would have to be set up to avoid any predetermination of guilt based on what has been written in the public domain. Of course, this is hardly a new challenge for the judicial system and the court is empowered to impose publication restrictions, to screen jury members, and even to move the location of a trial for this reason.

But Albrechtsen's reference to a "trial by Twitter" seems to imply a concern over something else entirely—not the right to a fair criminal trial, but a right to an untarnished reputation. This is quite a different matter.

It is true that public shaming by Twitter can exact tangible damage. Welsh journalist and author Jon Ronson wrote a book on the subject, and documented sustained economic and psychological harm from so-called "Twitter pile-ons." However, Ronson's concern focused on people who had engaged in a victimless breach of social mores. He also noted that the only people who escaped unscathed were men who were caught up in consensual sex scandals.

The fact is that we do have legal protections in place for people's reputation—the law of defamation. Indeed, Australian defamation laws are widely regarded as placing excessive emphasis on reputation protection at the expense of freedom of expression.

## The Real Legal Failure

Given this risk of being sued for defamation, it is worth examining why victims are turning to social media to hold perpetrators to account, since the rights of society and victims are theoretically promoted via the four (somewhat contradictory) aims of the criminal justice system.

These are:

- protection—keeping the public safe from offenders for a period of time;
- punishment—fulfilling the public desire to see retribution visited on offenders;
- deterrence—discouraging others from offending; and
- rehabilitation—helping criminals to better integrate and to make a positive contribution to society.

The problem is that the criminal justice system is particularly poor at achieving these outcomes for sexual harassment and assault. Consider the following statistics.

In a 2016 ABS Survey, one in two women (53% or 5 million) and one in four men (25% or 2.2 million) reported having experienced sexual harassment during their lifetime. A further one in five women (18% or 1.7 million) and one in 20 men (4.7% or 428,800) had experienced sexual violence since the age of 15. More significantly, nine out of ten women did not contact the police, and even those who do go to the police are statistically unlikely to see a conviction.

Across 2009-2010, for example, there were 7,066 incidents of alleged rape, indecent assault and/or incest recorded by Victoria Police. Of these, only 33.7% (or 2,381) resulted in prosecution, with just 23.3% (or 1,643) ending up in court. The Victoria report did not have complete data for conviction rates, but a similar NSW study from 2015 found that just 50.3% resulted in conviction and less than half of these resulted in a custodial sentence.

## A Voice for Victims

Beyond these statistics, there is also the fact that many victims find the system alienating and re-traumatising. Not only is their character and behaviour often placed on trial, but victims are often silenced by the justice system and denied the opportunity to shape the narrative of their own experience of assault. In light of these poor experiences and low likelihood of securing justice, it's clear why so many victims are seeking justice elsewhere.

And this is the key reason for #MeToo. It is a movement seeking an end to the culture of impunity that exists around sexual harassment and assault, and to demand that victims be given a voice in shaping the narrative of these crimes.

From this perspective, comments like Albrechtsen's are problematic because they serve to once again silence victims and to reassert the rights of perpetrators to be privileged within this narrative. The #MeToo movement is a symptom of the fundamental failures of our criminal justice system to protect the rights of victims. It might be uncomfortable, but that doesn't make it wrong.

> *"Those who level false accusations also cause damage to those who are truly abused because it puts their credibility in question."*

# False Accusations Hurt Real Victims

*Sarah Engel*

*In the following viewpoint, Sarah Engel looks at how the #MeToo movement affects teens and college students. She notes that a Georgia bill would prevent schools from investigating sexual assault claims unless the police were involved. The intent is to prevent schools from punishing students who have been falsely accused. However, the bill would force victims to suffer through the legal investigation, instead of allowing them other ways to complain. That could make sexual assault victims even less willing to step forward. VOXATL is an Atlanta site written by teens, for teens.*

As you read, consider the following questions:

1. How common are false accusations of sexual assault, according to the article?
2. How do false accusations hurt true victims of sexual assault?
3. How are teens learning about sex and sexual assault, according to the article?

This past year, every teenager's Twitter feed has been overflowing with sexual assault and rape accusations—especially toward the Hollywood elite. Since the Harvey Weinstein scandal in October 2017, people of all ages and genders have been sharing their traumatic experiences of sexual violence across social media. With help from the #MeToo movement, actors, producers and musicians to name a few have been revealed to be sexual predators. As a result, we've seen careers and personal lives ravaged by allegations of sexual harassment and violence. Harvey Weinstein, Matt Lauer, Kevin Spacey, Nev Shulman and Aziz Ansari are among the accused, and whose careers have suffered as a result. Weinstein was let go from his entertainment company, and Lauer and Spacey were released from their television contracts. Not to say that some of these individuals were undeserving of the backlash and consequences they received, but there is room for discussion as to whether or not all of the aforementioned people suffered prematurely.

In light of the collateral damage that often comes with the allegations, baseless accusations of sexual assault against other celebrities have also been spanning social media. Most notably, star of MTV's Catfish, Nev Shulman, was accused of sexual assault in May. Schulman denied the claims, but the show was suspended. Upon a later investigation, the claims were deemed not credible by MTV, and the show has since been reinstated. Teens on social media were quick to respond.

But false accusations of rape and sexual assault are not confined only to the entertainment industry. Professional athletes, CEOs and anyone in a position of authority are more likely to be falsely accused of sexual assault. In recent years, we've seen Brian Banks, former Atlanta Falcons linebacker, who in 2002 was accused of rape, served five years in prison and five years on parole, but was later exonerated when his accuser admitted she lied about being assaulted. Though his accuser's motives were never revealed, it was clearly a case of someone taking advantage of Banks' authority. I spoke with Lawrence Zimmerman, an Atlanta-based criminal justice lawyer who represents those under investigation of sexual assault. He commented: "A false allegation of a sexual nature is the most devastating allegation. They will lose their job immediately and the punishments are severe." Sharah Hutson, an Atlanta teen, described seeing these false accusations on her Instagram feed, and the implications that come with that: "When I see those accusations it's really scary to watch how that person gets immediately cut from their friend circle. Accountability and call-out culture online are kind of fuzzy and weird to me."

Georgia Tech has also been the subject of controversy recently, when two lawsuits were filed against Tech President Bud Peterson and other administrators by students who maintained they were unfairly forced to leave Tech after being accused of sexual assault. But an attempt at balance—Bill 51 being filed in the Georgia House of Representatives—may be doing more harm than good. Essentially, the bill prevents Georgia schools from investigating sexual assault claims unless police are involved. In effect, though, sexual assault victims are being denied their right to decide whether or not their experience is public record. This directly impacts current and perspective Georgia college students in taking away this right.

Rupkatha, an Atlanta teen who works with the Partnership Against Domestic Violence (PADV), stated that "there's already a huge misconception that most reported assaults are false, which is why people report most rape statistics as overblown. Because of the negative stigma associated with reporting sexual assault, a lot of times when you discuss statistics related to assault on college campuses, people will say that most of them are false accusations because people want attention, when in reality that's not the truth."

False accusations like Banks' and Schulman's take not only an emotional and financial toll on those accused, but also work to discredit actual survivors of rape and sexual assault. Zimmerman also stated that "False accusations are terrible for true victims. It makes everyone question whether or not a 'victim' is really a victim. Those who level false accusations also cause damage to those who are truly abused because it puts their credibility in question." Similarly, Rupkatha expressed that "There's always going to be an exception to any rule, unfortunately… It's just insulting and insensitive and rude to use such a gory and traumatizing situation to glorify yourself or gain some kind of upper-level advantage. I don't think it's right to say that all falsely reported sexual assaults are to glorify somebody's image either, but they take away from the victim's credibility regardless of intention. "

Another factor that plays a role in the culture of false accusations is media. Teens consuming information from movies and TV shows are being influenced by certain portrayals of sexual assault victims. The show "13 Reasons Why," for example, arguably sensationalizes the sexual assault of teens and, in depicting an unsuccessful trial of a rapist, furthers negative notions about survivors speaking out. On the other hand, Rupkatha mentioned how she appreciated representation in today's media.

"Fortunately, in the past decade, we've gotten a lot more exposure regarding taboo topics like sexual assault," she says. "There are alot of 'True American Crime Stories' that don't just discuss sexual assault against women but also against men."

Sharah, also recalled an article they'd recently read online that described the mental health of false accusers in a degrading way. She says, "It made me really scared and anxious that people were writing about this in that manner."

Rupkatha also stated, "This is the age where people are first experiencing intimate relationships and learning what consent means, and unfortunately in our schools right now, because of the current administration, sexual education has been defunded. I think we're obviously the demographic that's affected the most, and with more exposure from media, we're learning more about this, but I wish our schools would teach us."

Despite all of these false accusations, it's worth noting the fact that, according to the National Center for the Prosecution of Violence Against Women, only about 2-8% of all rape and sexual assault charges are proven to be false. This minority of accusations heavily distracts from the stories of actual victims of rape and sexual violence. In Rupkatha's own words, "Theoretically, we shouldn't let that small percentage affect the stories of millions of other people who've actually been affected by sexual assault. Just destigmatizing this idea of reporting sexual assault and discussing consent more would definitely impact us beneficially."

> *"How should feminists and proponents of the #metoo movement respond when one of their own is accused of sexual misconduct?"*

# It's About Power, Not Sex

*Kimberly Lawson*

*In the following viewpoint, Kimberly Lawson explores the role of power in sexual assault and harassment. She notes that several women, including feminists and leaders of the #MeToo movement, have been accused of sexual harassment or assault. In fact, the viewpoint notes, sexual harassment and assault are not about sex or gender. They are a way powerful people abuse those who are less powerful. Sources quoted say we should focus on changing society, not choosing whom to support and whom to blame. Kimberly Lawson is a freelance writer.*

As you read, consider the following questions:

1. Why were some women slow to believe #MeToo accusations against women?
2. What does the article mean by "There's no perfect victim"?
3. How does power tie into sexual assault, and what can society do about that?

"#MeToo Has Always Been About Power—Not Specific People," by Kimberly Lawson, Broadly, Vice Media, August 25, 2018. Reprinted by permission.

On Wednesday, actor and musician Jimmy Bennett spoke out on the allegations that Harvey Weinstein accuser Asia Argento had sexually assaulted him in 2013. He was 17 at the time when Argento, his co-star in the 2004 film *The Heart Is Deceitful Above All Things*, allegedly assaulted him in a California hotel. (The age of consent in California is 18.)

"I did not initially speak out about my story because I chose to handle it in private with the person who wronged me," Bennett, now 22, said in a statement. "My trauma resurfaced as she came out as a victim herself. I have not made a public statement in the past days and hours because I was ashamed and afraid to be part of the public narrative."

Bennett also said he "tried to seek justice in a way that made sense to me at the time because I was not ready to deal with the ramifications of my story becoming public." According to documents obtained by the *New York Times*, Argento agreed to quietly pay him $380,000 after he threatened in November—a month after Argento publicly accused Weinstein of rape—to sue her.

Argento, 42, has denied ever having a sexual relationship with Bennett, and said the decision to pay him was made at the time by her boyfriend Anthony Bourdain, who killed himself earlier this summer. After her statement came out, however, TMZ published a photo of Argento and Bennett and screenshots of text messages allegedly between her and a friend that suggested she did have sex with the teen.

The allegations against the Italian actress and director, who has emerged as a visible figure in the #metoo movement, surfaced just a week after a renowned feminist professor, New York University's Avital Ronell, was suspended for sexually harassing a male former graduate student. The *New York Times*' Zoe Greenberg reported that "a group of scholars from around the world, including prominent feminists," came to Ronell's defense, thus raising an important question many still struggle to answer: How should feminists and proponents of the #metoo movement respond when one of their own is accused of sexual misconduct?

It's something we've been grappling with for some time now. When Sen. Al Franken was accused of sexual harassment late last year, for example, a number of women publicly defended him, dubbing him "an honorable public servant." When former attorney general Eric Schneiderman was accused of physically and psychologically abusing several romantic partners, many looked back at his reputation as a staunch defender of women's rights.

And this week, when the *New York Times'* report on Argento first came out, Rose McGowan—another Weinstein accuser who's known for being a fierce critic of abuse in Hollywood—suggested people "[b]e gentle."

"None of us know the truth of the situation and I'm sure more will be revealed," she wrote in a tweet that's since been deleted.

Weinstein's attorney Ben Brafman also weighed in, noting that this recent development revealed "a stunning level of hypocrisy."

In fact, numerous media outlets have published thinkpiece after thinkpiece after thinkpiece this week exploring how Argento's shocking assault allegations could potentially impact the #metoo movement. Writer Danielle Tcholakian summarized some of her angst over Argento for the *Daily Beast* as such: "When Bennett's accusations first surfaced, I struggled. I had become so defensive of this woman I didn't even know, this stand-in for all the women whose stories I had listened to, stories I slaved over, taking forever to report, because I was determined not to let them experience the response she had gotten.

"There are no perfect victims, after all—the ones I spoke to were rarely an exception to that rule," Tcholakian continued. "The thing we talk about less often, but which is equally true, is that there are rarely perfect villains, either."

As many have pointed out, the #metoo movement—which launched in 2006 but gained widespread media attention recently with the sheer number of people coming forward to share their stories of being sexually abused by high-profile men—was never about any one individual. On Monday, #metoo founder Tarana Burke tweeted that this public reckoning with the way society deals with sexual violence and harassment "is less about crime & punishment and more about harm and harm reduction.

"It will continue to be jarring when we hear the names of some of our faves connected to sexual violence unless we shift from talking about individuals and begin to talk about power," she continued.

It's easy to get caught up in what's happening with one person who's been at the forefront of this movement, says Carly Mee, interim executive director at SurvJustice. "But it was never about just one person, it was about everyone," she tells Broadly. "The issue of sexual violence and sexual harassment isn't going away until we do something about it. And the focus should really be about reducing the overall harm that those issues cause survivors. It's about survivors as a whole."

But Mee admits she's not surprised by some of the conversations the allegations against Argento have ignited because society mostly still struggles to understand how nuanced sexual violence is. "We want to believe survivors, but then people are like, 'Well, that's messy because she's a survivor.' I think that's really the key point: There's no perfect victim. There can be survivors who also do really bad things on a number of levels."

Sexual violence happens in many different spheres to many different people, Mee continues. "We can't focus too much on defining victims versus perpetrators because it all blends together. We need to focus more on: here's this specific action that we can hold people accountable for, and how can we make larger policy changes to address this problem in the future."

Though the news of Argento's alleged behavior may be disheartening, Mee adds, it also serves as a reminder that we cannot idealize any one individual associated with this movement, no matter who they are.

In many ways, the biggest impact of the public outpouring of #metoo stories over the last nine months has offered people the language and courage they need to share their own experiences. Even Bennett said he was compelled to confront his alleged abuser after she came forward with her own #metoo story.

"Many survivors credit #MeToo [with] removing shame and stigma associated with their stories," says Amanda Nguyen, CEO and founder of national civil rights nonprofit Rise. "Though this has helped remove several barriers for survivors and has allowed them to make the first step toward finding justice and reconciliation, we still have a lot of work to do as a society. We've only just begun to open the door to reveal decades of systemic sexual violence and harassment that large institutions have covered up or turned a blind eye to."

Certainly, there has been a shift toward publicly holding some people accountable: Earlier this summer, for example, Weinstein was indicted on several sex crimes. At the same time, however, many people continue to support President Trump, who's been accused of sexual assault and harassment by at least 19 women; R. Kelly continues to tour nationally despite numerous allegations of abusing women and girls; and disgraced Fox News commentator Bill O'Reilly, who paid millions of dollars to settle various sexual harassment lawsuits, is still getting airtime.

Until serious repercussions are handed out across the board, advocates say there won't be real systemic change.

"As long as these perpetrators continue to hold positions of power and control, we have not started believing survivors or taken their stories and accusations seriously enough as a society," Nguyen says. "I am optimistic that this generation will see a world free from sexual violence, but in order for that to happen, we need to remove the power from the crime, which we have not yet accomplished. The best we can do to help prevent sexual violence is reform our laws." (Currently, Nguyen is working to pass the Sexual Assault Survivors' Bill of Rights in every state, which would guarantee equal protection under the law for survivors who have experienced sexual assault and, among other things, ensure rape kit procedures are fair and efficient.)

Mee agrees, pointing out that there are many other areas outside of Hollywood, including college campuses and labor industries, that have yet to garner similar attention when it comes to tackling these systemic issues. She points to Title IX policy changes enacted by Education Secretary Betsy DeVos as just one instance of how survivors at the campus level are being undermined. "I haven't heard many celebrities speaking out about that," Mee says.

Instead of focusing so much on how the allegations against one person within the movement will impact this work, Mee says she'd love to see these discussions evolve into more action. For example, one larger issue is that many universities are about to enter what survivor advocates call "The Red Zone"—the time of year in the fall freshman semester when campus sexual violence is most likely to occur.

"I think people need to pull their heads out of the sand and look around," Mee says, "because there are so many issues that are out there, and you just need to grab one."

> *"It's merely our job to take note, understand the power dynamics involved in sexual misconduct, and cheer for civil rights, justice, and equal protection under the law."*

# We Need to Hold Women Accountable, Too

*Deborah L. Davis*

*In the following viewpoint, Deborah L. Davis explores the case of a female New York University professor who was accused of sexual harassment by a male student. Many people rushed to defend the professor. Many of her defenders were feminists who generally supported the #MeToo movement. They seemed to feel that Title IX was meant to protect women, but not men. The author notes that abuse is about power. That can happen regardless of the gender identity or sexual orientation of the people involved. In this author's view, we must recognize that people we like and respect can do bad things, and we must hold them accountable. Deborah L. Davis, Ph.D. is a developmental psychologist and author.*

"#MeToo: Can a Feminist Be Guilty of Sexual Misconduct?" by Deborah L. Davis, *Psychology Today*, August 17, 2018. Reprinted by permission.

As you read, consider the following questions:

1. What makes the case described in this viewpoint unusual and controversial?
2. How are power dynamics more important than gender or gender identity when it comes to sexual harassment and abuse?
3. Should we treat people differently based on their sex, gender identity, or sexual orientation, according to this author?

Another #metoo claim came to light this week, when a Title IX report was leaked and a lawsuit was filed. The accuser is a former graduate student and the accused is a prominent NYU professor who is highly respected and world-renowned in the fields of philosophy and comparative literature. You've probably never heard of neither the student nor the professor, but because of multiple unusual twists, this case has become controversial and juicy fodder for news headlines, blogs, editorials, and of course, Twitter.

At first glance, this case looks typical. When the accused professor was investigated and suspended for sexual harassment, many colleagues rushed to this person's defense—not unlike the usual parade that happens when a powerful man falls from grace due to sexual misconduct, and his defenders can't believe it's true. And as per usual, this professor's defenders are blaming the student-victim as an untrustworthy liar, and are beseeching NYU to restore power and position to this person, because of such a stellar career. So what else is new?

Well, here are the twists that make this case so controversial: The former graduate student is a gay male; the professor is a woman who identifies as queer and feminist; the people rushing to her defense are like-minded colleagues and fans. These defenders are NOT misogynists or even social conservatives; they are prominent feminist theorists, philosophers, and intellectuals who pride themselves on critical thinking and supporting progressive ideals—such as victims seeking justice and being listened to, thanks to the #metoo movement. But by coming to the professor's defense, these colleagues appear to have let their own biases overpower their judgment. Some have even cried foul, arguing that Title IX, considered to be a feminist victory that protects girls and women, is wrongly being "twisted and turned around" to hold a woman accountable.

Say what?

Let's back up a little and get some context.

Title IX is a federal civil rights law that was passed in 1972, prohibiting sex discrimination in educational settings. Before Title IX, there were no laws protecting female students from unequal treatment with regard to recruitment, admission, financial aid, course offerings, or sexual harassment. Unfortunately, until the year 2000, when a new regulation made enforcement, reporting, and resolving complaints a priority, sexual harassment in particular remained rampant and largely unreported and/or not prosecuted, especially in universities. And without recourse, too many women have felt trapped in a system that didn't support their goals of getting an education and good grades without having to tolerate or fend off sexual advances. Now that administrations have clear procedures to follow, more students are being heard, more perpetrators are suffering the consequences, and justice is being served.

And indeed, the vast majority of cases do involve protecting female students from male perpetrators. But can Title IX, a major feminist victory, be invoked to protect a male student's rights in a case against a widely-respected woman who is a feminist scholar? A feminist who identifies as queer, no less? Accused of sexual harassment by a man who is gay? This just doesn't add up...or does it?

If this news story has got you twisted, consider these 10 facts about sexual misconduct, human nature, and the law:

## 1.

Sexual misconduct is about having power over someone, not just about sex. Take away the details about gender and sexual orientation and view it through the lens of "Professor imposes and demands sexual contact with student. Title IX used to seek justice."

Or even more to the point, "Person in a position of power imposes and demands sexual contact with a person in position of vulnerability. Justice is served." Shouldn't this be cause for celebration?

## 2.

This power dynamic is especially obvious when, as is often the case, the accused uses power plays to fend off accusations and reclaim former power. Power plays typically include relying on having higher status (the words displayed in parentheses being implied and contextually understood by others):

- "I am obviously innocent (because I am important, accomplished, powerful)."
- "My accuser was obviously willing (because I'm important, accomplished, powerful)."
- "It was just a flirty game we played. (I'm a winner; my accuser is being a sore loser.)"
- "My accuser can't be believed or trusted (because their status is lower than mine)."
- "My accuser is to blame, initiating sexual contact with me (not being smart enough to succeed, and/or hoping to get points/ favors/ passes from me)."

Sound familiar? Isn't this what the male power brokers have been saying to defend themselves? Shouldn't this woman's power posturing elicit our outrage as well?

## 3.

This power dynamic is also obvious when we look at the similar reasoning proposed by those who rush to her defense. They are using the same tactics of denial, disbelief, justification, and counter-accusations, which merely blame the accuser and ignore or downplay the evidence against the accused.

## 4.

Title IX is a civil rights law that protects all students against sex discrimination by anyone. Not just heterosexual, cisgender females against heterosexual, cisgender males. In fact, the purpose of Title IX is to protect the vulnerable against the powerful.

## 5.

Male and female students are afforded the protections of Title IX because, after all, males can be victims too. Catholic priests abusing altar boys; troop leaders abusing Boy Scouts; athletic coaches abusing male players; and yes, teachers abusing male students. Does it matter, the gender, sexual orientation, or gender identity of the accuser or the accused? Power dynamics are power dynamics across the board.

## 6.

Power dynamics make any relationship between student and teacher unequal, as teachers always have the upper hand, rightly exercising their power to cultivate order in the classroom, offer instruction, give homework and tests, and assign grades. And whenever teachers exercise their power inappropriately, including sexually, they are taking advantage of this dynamic, rendering the student especially vulnerable to mistreatment.

## 7.

Vulnerability can be experienced in many ways. For example, according to the evidence in this case, the male student says he found it difficult to loosen his professor's grip. He coveted an education from NYU. He had admired her work and was thrilled at the prospect of being her student. She became his academic adviser, but, with strings attached, as she also allegedly wanted intimacy. According to his complaint, she wielded her power to make or break him, by promising to either facilitate or ruin his goals, depending on whether he yielded to her demands. She was allegedly manipulative, aggressive, and reactive, and as is typical for victims in abusive relationships, he says he didn't want to fall into her disfavor and couldn't see a way out. In cases like this, when determining who's at fault, we must remember to look at the one who holds the power, not at the one who doesn't.

## 8.

Feminists are not immune to making power plays. Just because someone identifies as a feminist or stands for equal rights doesn't mean that they are incapable of wielding power over others. Again, according to the lawsuit, she used her power over him to have their relationship inappropriately serve her longings for affection and intimacy.

## 9.

Success in one area of life doesn't guarantee success in all areas. Just because someone is a world-renowned authority in their field, this doesn't mean that they can carefully think through every aspect of their emotional lives. According to the emails included in the lawsuit and the other corroborating evidence, she appeared to show a lack of awareness and sound judgment with regard to her relationship with this student.

## 10.

A person's reputation is only as good as their worst fault. Just because someone is well-respected and appears to have an excellent track record mentoring students, this doesn't mean they are incapable of sexual misconduct. And just because someone has made stellar contributions to their field, this doesn't mean that they should be allowed to carry on, uninterrupted, without consequences for misconduct.

What really happened? And what should come of the lawsuit? That's not for you and I to decide, nor even to cop an opinion. It's merely our job to take note, understand the power dynamics involved in sexual misconduct, and cheer for civil rights, justice, and equal protection under the law.

# Periodical and Internet Sources Bibliography

*The following articles have been selected to supplement the diverse views presented in this chapter.*

Nanette Asimov, "#MeToo Movement Spurs #HimToo Backlash: 'People Don't Want to Believe,'" *San Francisco Chronicle*, Oct. 13, 2018. https://www.sfchronicle.com/nation/article/MeToo-movement-spurs-HimToo-backlash-People-13304270.php.

Marcos Breton, "Does Innocent Until Proven Guilty Still Matter in the Age of #MeToo?" The *Sacramento Bee*, Dec. 8, 2017. https://www.sacbee.com/news/local/news-columns-blogs/marcos-breton/article188702284.html.

Taryn De Vere, "The Real Victims of #MeToo? Men." P.S. I Love You, July 13, 2018. https://psiloveyou.xyz/the-real-victims-of-metoo-men-9def6ae4f281.

Sady Doyle, "Despite What You May Have Heard, 'Believe Women' Has Never Meant 'Ignore Facts,'" *Elle* Magazine, Nov. 29, 2017. https://www.elle.com/culture/career-politics/a13977980/me-too-movement-false-accusations-believe-women/.

Jane Gilmore, "Presumption of Innocence and the #MeToo Backlash," The *Sydney Morning Herald*, Oct. 23, 2018. https://www.smh.com.au/lifestyle/life-and-relationships/presumption-of-innocence-and-the-metoo-backlash-20181019-p50aqw.html.

Janice Harper, "To Believe or Not Believe Bill Cosby's Accusers," *Psychology Today*, Nov. 24, 2014. https://www.psychologytoday.com/us/blog/beyond-bullying/201411/believe-or-not-believe-bill-cosbys-accusers.

Sarah Jaffe, "The Collective Power of #MeToo," *Dissent Magazine*, Spring 2018. https://www.dissentmagazine.org/article/collective-power-of-me-too-organizing-justice-patriarchy-class.

Laura Johnson, "Men Say They're Guilty Until Proven Innocent in #MeToo Era," Cleveland.com, Sep. 4, 2018. https://www.cleveland.com/shatter/2018/09/men_in_the_metoo_era_say_theyv.html.

Matt Kelly, "How to Undermine #MeToo," Radical Compliance, Oct 8, 2018. http://www.radicalcompliance.com/2018/10/08/undermine-metoo-allegations/.

David Robb, "Why Shamed #MeToo Scoundrels Are Getting Off the Legal Hook," Deadline, Sep. 5, 2018. https://deadline. com/2018/09/sexual-assault-hollywood-cases-no-prosecution-kevin-spacey-harvey-weinstein-steven-seagal-1202457117/.

Salil Tripathi, "How the #MeToo Movement Has Changed the Equation," Live Mint, Oct 18, 2018. https://www.livemint.com/Opinion/On399PdTjOMXrB1h9kcZyN/Opinion--How-the-MeToo-movement-has-changed-the-equation.html.

Bari Weiss, "The Limits of 'Believe All Women,'" *New York Times*, Nov. 28, 2017. https://www.nytimes.com/2017/11/28/opinion/metoo-sexual-harassment-believe-women.html.

Emily Yoffe, "The Problem with #Believe Survivors," *Atlantic*, Oct. 3, 2018. https://www.theatlantic.com/ideas/archive/2018/10/brett-kavanaugh-and-problem-believesurvivors/572083/.

OPPOSING
VIEWPOINTS®
SERIES

# CHAPTER 4

# How Will the #MeToo Movement Change the Future?

# Chapter Preface

Most people agree that the #MeToo movement has been a force for change in our culture. But where should we go from here? In this chapter, the viewpoint authors look to the future. One viewpoint notes that women have often been punished for speaking out against their abusers. This still happens, but perhaps we can go in a different direction in the future. We need to train girls to speak up when they are harassed. We need to share stories so men realize how common sexual harassment is. And we need to train boys to listen when girls and women speak.

Several authors point out that people we know and like can be guilty of sexual harassment. It's not enough to rejoice when men in power fall. We must fight sexism in society all around us. It is common in schools, in workplaces, and in society. Sometimes gender bias is so ingrained we don't even notice it. We can't fight problems if we haven't even recognize them. We need more conversations about gender roles, equality, and consent. We can and should support women in many ways.

One viewpoint notes that women can be guilty of sexual harassment and abuse. This can shock and upset those who want to use #MeToo to take down men in power. But if abuse is really about power, not sex, then we need to address the role power plays in sexual violence. Anyone can be an abuser, and anyone can be abused, regardless of their sex, gender identity, or sexual orientation. Until we hold everyone accountable for their actions, we cannot have a safe and fair world. It's not enough to have rules guiding relationships between teachers and students, or between coworkers. Rules won't be effective if they don't address power relationships.

People of color can be especially vulnerable to abuse. Black women have suffered a long history of sexual abuse. Even today, the police and government may treat them unfairly. Until the #MeToo movement fully supports everyone, we cannot have justice.

While it has shown substantial influence, the #MeToo movement is fairly new. Will people lose interest in the coming years? Or will they take the movement's momentum as an opportunity to change society? In this chapter, the viewpoint authors debate where we might go, and where we should go.

> *"If women own and unleash the power they have, in overt and subtle ways, the world will change."*

# We Can Make a Better Future

*Doyenne*

*In the following viewpoint, authors from Doyenne wonder about potential backlash from the #MeToo movement. The authors note that in the past, women have been punished for speaking out against their abusers. The authors believe that the present era can be different. They list ways people can support women and ensure they are not beaten down by #MeToo backlash. In these authors' view, women and their male allies should take the lead in changing the world. That way, they can counteract negative backlash. Doyenne is an organization that helps entrepreneurial women.*

As you read, consider the following questions:

1. How can people support women, according to the authors?
2. How can white women better support women of color, according to the viewpoint?
3. What is involved in treating men like adults, according to the authors?

"Be the Backlash to the #MeToo Movement," Doyenne, January 15, 2018. Reprinted by permission.

2017 was the year of #MeToo.

2018, according to some pundits, will be the year of the Backlash. They say women will pay the price for bringing down so many men of power through sexual harassment allegations.

This conversation absolutely infuriates me.

But the idea is also not without precedent.

There's nothing new about women being punished for speaking the truth about men's behavior.

When I was in college, back in the 1990's, Clarence Thomas was being approved to serve on the U.S. Supreme Court. For those of you too young to remember, a very familiar scene played out. Anita Hill, with reluctance, came forward and shared her story: Thomas, her boss, had sexually harassed her throughout her tenure at the Department of Education's Office of Civil Rights and then at the Equal Employment Opportunity Commission. Thomas denied all claims.

Back then, the backlash was real. Hill was villainized and then Sen. Joe Biden prevented three additional women from testifying against Thomas, saying it wouldn't be appropriate for Supreme Court confirmation hearings. He used his power to stop women from telling their stories publicly and demonstrating a pattern of behavior by Thomas.

So where are we now? We're having the same damn conversations. It's time to change that.

The backlash forecasters expect to see more men making claims like the one Mike Pence did, when he said that he refuses to eat a meal alone with a woman who is not his wife.

They suggest women should expect threats and actions that limit women's access to career building meetings and relationships, because of men's perceived threat of getting accused of sexual harassment.

What does it say if a man says he won't be alone in a room with a woman anymore because it's too risky? It either means that he knows he can't control himself and thinks he's going to do something out of bounds, or it means he believes that women are liars, women are vindictive, and women must be controlled.

The underlying narrative of this backlash concept is that poor, innocent men are going to be accused of things because of "nasty" women. This narrative is old, tired, and needs to end.

If you've been warning women about their impending doom as a result of the #MeToo movement, JUST STOP.

Unfortunately, it's not just men who are warning women about a backlash. Women of all ages have made similar comments. When we, as women, caution other women not to use their voice for fear of repercussions, we do the work of the patriarchy. Men don't have to say anything to silence women—other women do the work for them. It's defeatist, and it's a self-fulfilling prophecy.

The question in my mind is how 2018 will differ from 1991. Twenty-seven years have passed. What is different today? Part of me is furious that things haven't changed; men are still doing this s\*\*\* and are rarely held accountable. But, another part of me is fully vibrating with the idea that things have changed, or at least changed enough. That this is a moment in history when women, together, can create a new game, with new rules. Rules that no longer tolerate the overt and subtle ways women are shut out of the system.

We need to be the f\*\*\*ing backlash, not just sit here waiting for the backlash against us.

But what does it take to do this? I will share with you what I am working on:

1. Let's look deeply at the power we hold, both individually and collectively, and use it. I invite you to join me in assessing your own sources of power. What do you know, who do you know, in what settings and through what channels do you have voice, what dollars do you have and where do you deploy them? When can you backup another woman in a meeting or at an event, recommend or even hire a woman for a job, promote a woman to

leadership, nominate a woman for an award, or encourage her to run for office?

2. Let's find ways to recognize and honor the diverse life experiences of women. We are not all the same and we don't have to be. Specifically, there is a history of white women including women of color when it serves us, and excluding them the minute it doesn't. A history of prioritizing white women's needs over the needs of women of color. White women need to look at how we have used our power in ways that significantly hurt and undermine other women. We must find pathways forward—pathways in which our differences strengthen us and don't divide us.

3. Let's begin to treat men like the grown-ass adults they should be. I can't tell you all the conversations I have in which women are exerting tremendous amounts of energy to coddle fragile male egos. We choose our words carefully. We let things slide, whether its insults or assaults. We accept mediocre work. We don't call them out in meetings. We let them take the credit for ideas, work, and successes they aren't responsible for. We let them talk so they can feel important. We let them have the title, salary, perks they demand, whether they earned them or not. We figure out ways, behind the scenes, to make their dumb-ass ideas work. And, we need to stop. They are grown men—not children. We are not their mothers. We are not their keepers.

To all the men who have chosen to read this post, thank you. Thank you for identifying it as relevant to you. Thank you for reading to this point. And, please, continue reading even if you are uncomfortable. Forward progress depends on it. Stand beside us. Take risks with us.

The #MeToo campaign, seriously, is only the tip of the iceberg. If women own and unleash the power they have, in overt and subtle ways, the world will change.

Women, don't let yourself be silenced by men who can't handle the truth. It's time to BE THE BACKLASH. Continue to hold men accountable for their actions, and don't let them cut you out of their meetings, their boardrooms, or their happy hours. Call them on that bull**** yourself and support other women who do it, too.

This movement is so long overdue. We cannot afford to let it stop when the hashtag flames out.

I have an 11-year-old daughter. When I look at her, I wonder, "Is she going to have the same issues that we have now when she enters the workforce? Will her generation still be fighting for legitimacy?"

We cannot let another generation go by. The only thing that's going to save the planet is women gaining more power and exercising the power they have. So go out there and be the backlash.

> *"Black women were subjected to violent sexual abuse and forced nudity as routine social practice, in ways that would have been unthinkable toward white women."*

# #MeToo Needs to Support Black Women Better

*Yolonda Wilson*

*In the following viewpoint Yolonda Wilson explores the ways black women have experienced sexual violence. They may suffer different assaults than white women. The author notes that black women have often been seen as less moral and less sensitive to pain. This allowed white people in power to abuse black women in a variety of ways. Even today, black women are given less privacy, safety, and respect by the police. In this author's view, understanding this is necessary to stop sexual violence. The #MeToo movement needs to know how black women have been treated historically and the special threats they face today. Yolonda Wilson is assistant professor of philosophy at Howard University in Washington, D.C.*

As you read, consider the following questions:

1.  How have black women's bodies and sexuality been viewed differently from those of white women, throughout history?
2.  How does the government permit sexual violence against black women?
3.  Why does this author feel that the unusual forms of sexual violence black women suffer are relevant to the #MeToo movement?

In April, a 25-year-old black woman named Chikesia Clemons was violently arrested by police at a Waffle House restaurant in Alabama.

A video of the arrest that went viral shows police pulling Clemons from her chair and throwing her to the floor. In the process, her breasts are exposed and her dress rides up in the back. When she attempts to cover her breasts, the two officers on top of her threaten to break her arm for "resisting."

Clemons' experience is not unique. In the U.S., black women are not afforded the same regard for bodily privacy as white women.

Another example: In an investigation of the Baltimore City Police Department, the Department of Justice found that the Baltimore Police Department frequently engaged in unjustified strip searches of African-Americans. In one instance, Baltimore police conducted a strip search of a black woman, including an anal cavity search, on a sidewalk in broad daylight and in full public view. The woman's pleas to not be forced to disrobe in public were ignored. Her offense? A broken headlight.

While the #MeToo movement has been successful in bringing down several high-profile assailants, critics continue to argue that it has been monopolized by middle- and upper-class white women, particularly white Hollywood actresses. This, despite the fact that a black woman, Tarana Burke, created the Me Too campaign more than a decade ago. These criticisms reflect the fact that black women have experienced sexual violence differently than white women.

As a philosopher of race and gender who has written about sexual harassment, I offer historical context on the ways that black women experience sexual abuse, often by the authority of the state, as a way to think about black women's contemporary experiences as the kinds of experiences that #MeToo should address.

## History of Black Women's Bodies on Display

As early as the 17th century, European men wrote travel narratives about their trips to West Africa to capture, enslave and trade African people. Their writings offer a window into how they perceived African women and what they thought primarily European male readers would find titillating.

In particular, their descriptions of West African women's style of dance played a role in shaping European perceptions of black women's sexual immorality and availability.

These travel accounts were the popular media of their day and offered some of the first reports of continental Africa to average Europeans. For example, Frenchman Jean Barbot wrote of African men and women "knocking bellies together very indecently" while "uttering some dirty mysterious words." Meanwhile, naval officer Abraham Duqesne characterized African women as desiring the "caresses of white men."

Because African women differed from European women both in attire and bodily movement, European travel writers regarded African women as sexually available and immoral. European settlers carried these attitudes to the United States where enslaved black women were subjected to violent sexual abuse and forced nudity as routine social practice, in ways that would have been unthinkable toward white women.

## WHAT'S NEXT FOR THE #MeToo MOVEMENT?

What's next for the MeToo movement? At the Council of Europe's annual World Forum for Democracy—which this year is focused on gender equality—we asked activists one simple question.

### Shiori Ito, Japan, freelance journalist

[In Japan] we're never taught what consent means. We live in a society where no sometimes means yes and how can we cope with that? We set our consent age as 13 years old and they don't teach what consent is in school.

Only 4% of rape is reported to the police. 96% doesn't exist, it's not there. Why? A lot of it is to do with the judicial system and how they handle the investigation, what kind of culture or idea they have against rape.

### Diana Bologova, Germany, European Youth Press

This is very important, and that actually concerns every single girl, every single woman, and we have to go on.

And when I heard that this whole forum was based on that campaign and it was inspired by this campaign, I did everything to come here.

## Sexual Violence and the Father of Gynecology

By the 19th century, treating black and white women differently was firmly entrenched in society. Nowhere was this more evident than in the practice of J. Marion Sims, the physician widely regarded by gynecologists as the "father of modern gynecology." The convention of the period was for physicians to conduct gynecological examinations of white women with averted gazes while the patients remained as clothed as possible.

However, Sims also conducted medical experiments on enslaved black women that ultimately resulted in a technique to repair vesicovaginal fistula, an opening that can develop between

## Joycia Thorat, India, the Church's Auxiliary for Social Action

In India the main issue is that the MeToo movement is more limited to the upper class... Many times the experiences of violence against the Dalits or tribal children do not come out. They don't have the media, they don't have the social network, they don't have the social means, the capacity, the power.

Recently we had a story of a 13-year-old young child girl who was killed because she said no to a man. Her neighbour was from the upper caste. She was a Dalit child. But no press, no paper, no-one, no judiciary, no governance system, wanted to mention the case.

## Carola De Min, Italy, Council of Europe

We need the authorities, the policemen and other systems to trust women and to know how to handle the cases because at the moment they don't know. If the victims are asked what were you wearing, were you drunk, if someone says they were sexually harassed, for the most part, most of the time, it's true.

The first step has to be education. Also to keep talking about it, and social media has a role here... because not talking about it will make it a taboo, which will enlarge the problem.

"What's Next for the MeToo Movement?" by Sophie Hemery, opendemocracy .net, November 21, 2018.

the vaginal wall and the bladder or large intestine, sometimes as a result of childbirth. The enslaved black women were stripped completely naked and examined on all fours, as Sims and other physicians took turns using a specially created speculum that enabled full viewing of the vagina. Private citizens were also allowed to watch these experiments and they, too, were invited to witness the full exposure of enslaved women's vaginas.

Sims conducted his experiments without anesthesia, despite the fact that ether was known and in use by the time he performed later surgeries. Black women were denied anesthesia on the grounds that black people did not feel pain in the same ways that white people felt pain, a perception that still exists today. For example, one study found that when people viewed images of blacks receiving painful stimuli, like needle pricks, they responded with less empathy than when they viewed similar images of white people in pain.

## Sexual Violence in a Court of Law

In New York in 1925, another historical example shows how black women's exposed bodies have been treated with indifference. Kip Rhinelander, a member of New York's high society, was set to wed Alice Beatrice Jones, a working-class biracial woman. Their union drew national attention.

Although New York did not legally prohibit interracial marriage as other states did at that time, society strongly disapproved of interracial marriage.

Once their marriage was made public, Kip filed for divorce on the grounds of fraud. The salient question in the divorce hearing was whether Kip knew that Alice was black at the time of their marriage.

In order to answer that question, Alice's attorney suggested that Alice bare her breasts in front of the all-white male jury, judge and attorneys in order to prove her racial identity. By viewing the shading of her areolas and legs, he said, the jurors could assess whether Kip—who had admitted to premarital sex with her—should have known her racial identity.

The judge directed Alice to follow through. Neither Alice Rhinelander's tears nor her connection to a prominent white family could save her from the indignity of forced nudity in front of strangers. Ultimately, the jury decided that Alice was, in fact, "of colored blood" and that she did not conceal or misrepresent her racial identity.

## The Past Is Present

The hostility to black women's bodily privacy and dignity in these examples isn't accidental. Rather, it is part of the history of how black women have been cast in US society.

In the Sims and Rhinelander examples, the legal status of enslavement and weight of the court validated the coercive display of black women's bodies. The Department of Justice found that the Baltimore police used the weight of their badges to force compliance with public strip searches. Likewise, in the Waffle House example, although Clemons' initial exposure may not have been intentional, the police responded to her cries and her attempts to cover herself by using their authority to threaten her with further harm.

This is a unique form of sexual violence experienced by black women. The convergence of race and gender in black women's lives has created the social conditions in which black women are coerced and often expected, under threat of punishment by the government, to suffer the exposure of intimate body parts.

Race and gender converge in black women's lives and have created the social conditions under which black women are coerced and expected to suffer the exposure of intimate body parts, or else face punishment. If movements like #MeToo are serious about combating sexual violence, then they have to also understand these practices as sexual violence.

> "*The power to be heard has inspired other women to start networks and hashtags of their own, like #Doyna (meaning "That's enough) to challenge Senegal's silence on gender-based violence and harassment.*"

# The #MeToo Movement Should Listen to the Silence of Women in Africa

*Lynsey Chutel*

*In the following viewpoint Lynsey Chutel argues that, even in Africa, movements like #MeToo have benefitted mostly those of privilege. While the #MeToo movement in the United States has inspired similar movements in Africa, there is still much work to be done to stop the culture of harrassment, violence, inequality, and silence in even the most Western-influenced areas. Still, the author notes that the movement is an important path to progress for women, and it will be even more powerful if it includes women across all economic, racial, and geographic lines. Lynsey Chutel covers southern Africa from Johannesburg for Quartz. She previously worked as a correspondent for the Associated Press.*

As you read, consider the following questions:

1. Why did the #MeToo movement fail to take off in 2006, according to the author?
2. What double standard does the author expose using the example of a female presidential candidate in Rwanda?
3. What examples does the author provide of progress for women in Africa?

It seems that Africa's women have missed the chance to add their voices to the global phenomenon that the #MeToo moment became in 2018. Their relative silence is both a lesson in the movement's failure to become a truly inclusive network and a reminder of where power resides in patriarchal societies.

Through millions of tweets, the #MeToo movement created a safe space for women to come forward about the sexual harassment and sexual violence they had experienced. Since 2017, their collective voices and support brought down big Hollywood names, shook America's elite media circles, and forced other industries to take a closer look at how the women within their ranks were treated.

In just over a year, #MeToo has become a seminal moment in feminism. And yet, its current manifestation threatens to overlook the women this movement was started for. Tarana Burke founded the Me Too movement in 2006, as a way for black and low-income American women in particular to discuss sexual violence. She wanted to create a network and community of survivors and their allies, creating a curriculum to guide their advocacy, while searching for resources to support this program.

But it was only when actress Alyssa Milano tweeted the hashtag more than a decade later that it become the phenomenon the world knows now. It was meant as a personal gesture that quickly grew into a global movement, by social media mapping anyway. The idea was that if each woman who had experienced sexual harassment just tweeted the hashtag, the world would begin to understand the magnitude of the problem.

Now, in this form, the organization has international impact, creating the links that Burke first envisioned. While not initially connected to its originator, Milano acknowledged Burke and still works with her. Burke remains at the helm of the movement that has raised her own profile, and uses the accompanying accolades to spotlight the women of color for whom this movement was created.

And yet, it's impossible to ignore the fact that the reason the movement in its current form gained such momentum was because it was driven by mainly white, wealthy women who already had access to the platform and power needed. For all its victories, #MeToo has exposed divisions within the feminist movement.

Initially, the division was simultaneously ideological and generational, but then it became clear that women of color and lower-income women were being left out of the conversation. To its credit the #MeToo movement has tried to emphasize intersectionality—how social structures affect the different sections of one's identity, like race and gender—but because it is a movement that requires women to come forward on a public platform, it demands a certain amount of power on the part of its participants.

This is a power the majority of African women and others outside of the US simply don't have. And yet, India offered a glimmer of hope. Using the same hashtag, Indian women in particular were able to mobilize against misogyny in Bollywood, the media and the tech industry. Still, in India the movement carried the same burdens. India, like much of Africa, is an unequal society in which parts of the country resemble the West's progress, while impoverished and isolated women continue to suffer. Africa's attempts at a MeToo moment were similarly stop-start and privileged.

Last year, before #MeToo took off, there seemed to be the beginning of a reckoning, as Kenya's iconic tech company Ushahidi had to deal with sexual harassment claims head on. Even as the #MeToo wave grew, Kenya's reckoning did not move beyond this relatively new industry, illustrating how entrenched patriarchy is in other sectors of society.

South Africa, Africa's most advanced economy, tried to keep up with the international #MeToo trend, but like the US it privileged the voices of the wealthy. And when some women came forward to expose sexual harassment in corporate South Africa, some organizations chose to protect the perpetrators. Internal investigations and industry-specific protests did little to change office culture in a country where women and men have reported high levels of sexual harassment in the workplace.

If anything, sex scandals continued to be used by factions within the ruling party to attack the political careers of powerful men, with women as collateral damage. As the most recent sexual harassment allegations in the African National Congress show, the scandals did little to change the culture in the party that decides South Africa's policies.

And yet, as was the case with Rwandan independent presidential candidate Diane Rwigara, sexual harassment is an effective tool in trying to end the career of a female politician. Weeks after Rwigara announced her intention to run against president Paul Kagame in last year's election, nude photos of her were leaked and seen across the region. When that didn't deter her, the state charged the 37-year old businesswoman with fraud, barring her from contesting.

Nigerian academia is a microcosm for how sexual harassment falls through the social cracks, with perpetrators protected by their prestige. The recent conviction of a professor became a national story, and an example that not enough is done to protect women on and off campus. Still, even these are examples of how gender discrimination affects privileged women, with much less attention given to lower-income women.

African women and activists were clearly inspired by the US movement. In Senegal, where speaking out about abuse is discouraged and women are hushed by social requirements of respectability and feminine patience, two young women started #Nopiwouma. Meaning "I will not shut up" in Wolof, the hashtag goes further by creating an anonymous Google form that allows them to share their experiences. The power to be heard has inspired other women to start networks and hashtags of their own, like #Doyna (meaning "That's enough) to challenge Senegal's silence on gender-based violence and harassment.

Women's experiences across the continent are diverse and creating a comprehensive cross-continental picture is impossible, but the manner in which the African Union handled its own #MeToo moment shows just how low the standard is. In January 2018, women staffers appealed to senior officials to end gender discrimination in the AU. The matter was practically ignored until it reached the media in May. When it was finally dealt with, the AU found that the organization's most vulnerable, idealistic young interns and volunteers hoping for permanent work were targeted, but little could be done to protect them.

While there is still much work to do across Africa, much already has been done. In the last decade, a number of African states have begun passing legislation to protect women against gendered injustices like child marriage and domestic violence. Still, these new laws are only the start: the World Economic Forum found that it will take 135 years to close the gender gap in sub-Saharan Africa, mainly due to a lack of economic and political empowerment.

The attempts at recreating the #MeToo movement here, and the disappointing policy responses illustrate that even when African women try to speak up, societal pressures drown out their voices. Autonomous, empowered forums for women, like #MeToo, can speed up that process, but those movements need to be inclusive.

Despite criticism against it, the #MeToo movement is a much-needed moment in women's history and feminism. However, like previous waves that reverberated around the world, from the early 20th century Suffrage Movement to Sheryl Sandberg's Lean In, it also threatens to leave behind women of color and the poor, while privileging the experiences of usually white women. Reaching out across class, race and even geographic divides could make this a truly global movement.

African women are facing varying scales of discrimination all at once—from rape as a weapon of war in the hinterlands of some countries to jobs for sex within the urban skyscrapers. No single movement can solve all of these myriad challenges, but #MeToo can start by including their experiences and empowering women in these environments to speak up. It should apply the same principle to the women left behind everywhere.

If it seems like a lot to ask, just look at how much the movement has achieved since Milano's October 2017 tweet. Any movement that wants to protect women should make an extra effort to listen to the women who are too afraid to speak up.

> "Sexual harassment is often, in my view, a subcategory of bullying, and the attempt to address one without the other is doomed to fail."

# #MeToo Needs to Address Power

*Claire Potter*

*In the following viewpoint Claire Potter addresses sexual harassment and assault as the abuse of power. The author suggests that the #MeToo movement has primarily treated accusations as sexual. Yet workplaces have many relationships where power can be unbalanced. This is especially true at universities. People can abuse their power through sexual harassment or assault. When people see harassment and abuse purely as sex, they try to police it by stating rules for sexual relationships. Those rules cannot be effective if they don't consider power relationships, according to the author. Claire Potter is professor of history at the New School, New York.*

"A Lot of Things Are Broken: Why Focusing on Sex Won't Fix Sexual Harassment," by Claire Potter, Eurozine, January 26, 2018. Reprinted by permission.

As you read, consider the following questions:

1. Why does the author believe it is wrong to focus on rules for sex when trying to stop sexual harassment?
2. How can sexual harassment be a form of bullying, according to the viewpoint?
3. Why are mentoring relationships at colleges and in workplaces important? How can this lead to sexual harassment?

Back in the 1970s, radical feminists in the United States like Susan Brownmiller, Andrea Dworkin and Catharine MacKinnon, women who theorized rape and sexual harassment, had a valuable message: it wasn't about sex, but about power. So why do we persist in treating the revelations of the #MeToo movement as primarily sexual?

My own workplace is a university, where power hierarchies and potential arenas of sexual danger overlap. We emphasize the boundary that ought to exist between teachers and students, but neglect other relationships: between academic and administrative staff; support and janitorial staff and their supervisors; graduate students who are teaching assistants and undergraduates; athletic staff and athletes; tenured and untenured faculty; full-time and part-time, contingent or post-doctoral faculty. There are so many different sites of potential power imbalance that the idea of regulating them all is daunting.

So, we try, we wake up a couple of decades later, and we ask why we have failed. Again.

Ironically, movements like #MeToo merely enhance the policing of sex when what we need is greater insight into the nature of power. At my university, one of the functions of sexual harassment training is to teach us how to do this effectively and legally. Training is focused almost exclusively on our legal responsibilities under Title IX, a 1972 amendment to the Higher Education Act of 1965 which

## INTERVIEW WITH JENNIFER FREYD, PROFESSOR OF PSYCHOLOGY, ON THE FUTURE OF THE #MeToo MOVEMENT

### What terms do you think, or hope, the #MeToo Movement will popularize?

Betrayal trauma is [...] the particular bind that people get into when they're mistreated by someone they depend upon or trust. This leads to some amount of unawareness of the betrayal in order to protect the necessary relationship. I call this betrayal blindness. Betrayal, our research and others' has shown, is really damaging to the body and mind. Institutional betrayal extends this concept from a one-on-one relationship to something where a person is depending on the institution mistreating them.

### How can we properly punish perpetrators of sexual harassment?

There are 10 steps institutions can take to reduce institutional betrayal and promote institutional courage, the opposite. One is to incentivize whistleblowing. People can get rewarded. There could be a committee to reward them with a salary. It's not a crazy idea. Some industries like technology pay people to find bugs, and they get paid really well.

mandates gender equity in any educational programme receiving federal financial assistance.

What is interesting is that our trainings are not focused on the causes and consequences of sexual harassment. Nor do they address the nature and consequences of power, and how power is expressed and enforced through sexuality. Instead, they focus on prohibition. The idea is that if we all understood and enforced the rules about sex, we could eliminate the abuse of power.

DARVO, which stands for deny, attack and reverse victim and offender, is often used to describe the accused's reactions. What's the basis of this term?

But here's a whole pattern of [perpetrators] attacking the victim, calling them crazy or a liar and then saying, "I'm the victim, you're ruining my reputation." It's that pattern that raises a red flag of someone's responsibility. DARVO itself is harmful. It causes the victim to blame herself, and women are more likely to get DARVOed. Thing is, an innocent person doesn't need to attack the accuser and would be more interested in promoting evidence of their innocence.

Do you expect a backlash to the #Metoo Movement?

I do expect a significant backlash. Some elements are already present, with people saying the pendulum has swung too far. There are too many men getting accused, and men will be afraid to go to work. I imagine it'll get worse, and I expect a lot more DARVO, accusing the women of being the offenders. We should be prepared for that and call it out when it happens.

I'm hoping we've passed some tipping point, and I kind of think we have. It seems there was attention on military sexual trauma in 2010 and college sexual assault in 2013. The Obama administration in 2014 made it a priority and now this. That's a lot to happen in rapid succession.

"Will there be a Backlash to #MeToo?" by Libby Coleman, OZY, January 15, 2018.

I think this is terribly wrongheaded. Sexual harassment is often, in my view, a subcategory of bullying, and the attempt to address one without the other is doomed to fail. In fact, it has failed. Forty-five years after the passage of Title IX, and almost 40 years after Alexander v. Yale (a lawsuit which Yale won, but which also established the term "sexual harassment" in the law), sexist bullying in universities seems to be as pervasive as ever.

Universities aren't unique. In the film industry, where the tidal wave of #MeToo revelations began last fall, it is over sixty years since Marilyn Monroe reportedly announced to the Hollywood press, after signing her first major film deal: 'I'll never have to s*** another c*** in this town again.' (In another version of this story, she winks and adds: 'unless I want to, of course.') Yet that sexual act, and others, still seem to be a key point of entry into a media career.

In the industry I know best, education, we live with a dual reality: that people are not supposed to be having sexual relations with subordinates, and that they do all the time. Like the more high-profile media cases, the #MeToo moment in academia has been an opportunity to express our outrage at the miscreants who create chaos in the wake of their sexual affairs, and to reiterate our generally specious belief that universities would run smoothly if only the rules and ethical obligations about intimacy were clear and enforceable.

Enter Human Resources, the corporation counsel and a consultant or two to rectify the problem. Once a year we learn how to identify and report. We are reminded about the importance of confidentiality, and about how to respond to everything we might observe that is out of order: rape, groping, gossip about a student's sexual identity, stalking and comments about appearance, to name a few.

These trainings may well play a role in making us more self-aware and alleviating the inappropriate eroticization of our relationships. But I don't think they do much to address the ethical and moral complexities of a workplace where the personal power to help or harm individuals is so critical to advancing, or stalling, careers.

Important as it has been, the #MeToo moment has two flaws: the first is the assumption that the misuse of sex, rather than bullying and the misuse of power, is the source of harm and trauma in a sexual harassment case. The second is, well, the highly American focus on "me." Recently, a valued colleague noted that her hesitation over a proposed prohibition of sexual relationships between faculty and students was not because it was impossible (this is my reservation), but because of her own, rewarding, affair with a professor. This reluctance to accept that there is something much bigger at stake in a sexual harassment case, something that is in the nature of the institution and not the individual, is common.

Some American feminists go further than my hesitant colleague. They have (courageously in my view, because the reaction is often vicious) proposed that the sexual harassment cases, investigated under Title IX since 2013, can conceal the agency of the subordinate partner. For example, Laura Kipnis's book, *Unwanted Advances: Sexual Paranoia Comes to Campus* (2017), examines a case at her own university in which a student realized that an affair with a professor was actually sexual harassment only after extensive meetings with a Title IX investigator.

Kipnis has been criticized for her reporting on this case, which I have responded to elsewhere. But Kipnis's detailed narrative about her colleague also reveals what many sexual harassment trainings do not: that the everyday blurring of boundaries—the need students sometimes have for privacy during office hours; mentoring of colleagues and students; conferences; lab work; inviting students and colleagues for a social call in one's home or a restaurant; and receptions after talks—is actually inherent to the practice of higher education. So is picking out favoured students for an invitation-only conference: in some of the academic #MeToo cases, graduate students were invited to attend an exclusive event with a mentor, only to learn that they were expected to share a hotel room.

Here, we might want to return to "B*** J** City," as Hollywood was called in Marilyn Monroe's day, for a few lessons about how workplace cultures incubate bullying and exploitation. In October 2017, the actress Lupita Nyong'o wrote an op-ed about her own painful encounter with the catalyst for the #MeToo movement, film mogul Harvey Weinstein. It was a classic quid pro quo or "pay to play" situation: Nyong'o's potential reward would be a potential role; her punishment, should she refuse, the threat that she would never work at all. Nyong'o describes being socially, and sometimes physically, trapped by Weinstein, which she navigated either by setting boundaries, or blurring them when necessary. But, as she explains, in the performing arts, "the intimate is often professional and so the lines are blurred."

When lines are blurred, it's no wonder that simply making rules and expecting people to obey them fails. Shouldn't we consider, instead, how we might inhabit these liminal spaces ethically? Could we not learn more about why the power imbalances in our workplaces make some people so vulnerable and spare others? Discussions that have accompanied the #MeToo movement reveal the under-analysed fact that a vulgar or unwanted action that one person might perceive as navigable, or even insignificant, may be a traumatic snare for another. Sex is only one part of the formula for abusing authority and power. But the failure to address this fact also reveals how confused we are in the United States about what kind of currency sex represents in workplaces that are actually structured around intimate hierarchies of authority.

Which is why, perhaps, an effective #MeToo movement would stop talking about sex and start talking about the workplace itself, as well as what kinds of values are cultivated there. A former employee on the *Charlie Rose Show* told me, after Rose's career and the show were destroyed last year amidst accusations of sexual harassment going back years: "I've decided to take a step back from media, which has proven to be a pretty toxic environment for me personally in the last few years. I still love it," she said, "but it's become obvious that the issues in the industry go well beyond sexual harassment and abuse. The endless layoffs and reorganizations, the stillborn 'pivot to video,' the bleak native platform ecosystem that allows for the proliferation of wildly dishonest theories and ideologies posing as 'news,' and the by-line hero culture. A lot of things are broken." A lot of things are broken in universities too: and when our only focus is sex, we can't begin to fix them.

> "We may ache for gender equality
> but we're rarely framing or fighting
> for it in the same ways we fight for
> racial equality."

# Women Need to Speak Loudly and Be Tough

*Barbara Kingsolver*

*In the following viewpoint, Barbara Kingsolver urges women to fight sexism. She argues that society encourages men to be sexually aggressive. It encourages women to see male attention as flattery. That makes it hard for girls and women to tell boys and men when they don't like the type of attention they're getting. The author suggests that most women don't fight for gender equality the way they fight for racial equality. She gives examples of how society accepts gender inequality with few questions. Then she suggests that women should be clear and strong in their demands, as sweetness will not stop men or dismantle rape culture. Barbara Kingsolver is an American novelist.*

"#MeToo Isn't Enough. Now Women Need to Get Ugly," by Barbara Kingsolver, Guardian News and Media Limited, January 16, 2016. Reprinted by permission.

As you read, consider the following questions:

1. Why is it often hard for women to turn down male attention, according to the author?
2. What is the author's complaint with women changing their names when they marry?
3. Why does this author thinks people don't fight for gender equality the same way they fight for racial equality?

In each of my daughters' lives came the day in fifth grade when we had to sit on her bed and practise. I pretended to be the boy in class who was making her sick with dread. She had to look right at me and repeat the words until they felt possible, if not easy: "Don't say that to me. Don't do that to me. I hate it." As much as I wanted to knock heads around, I knew the only real solution was to arm a daughter for self-defence. But why was it so hard to put teeth into that defence? Why does it come more naturally to smile through clenched teeth and say "Oh, stop," in the mollifying tone so regularly, infuriatingly mistaken for flirtation?

Women my age could answer that we were raised that way. We've done better with our daughters but still find ourselves right here, where male puberty opens a lifelong season of sexual aggression, and girls struggle for the voice to call it off. The *Mad Men* cliche of the boss cornering his besotted secretary is the modern cliche of the pop icon with his adulating, naked-ish harem in a story that never changes: attracting male attention is a woman's success. Rejecting it feels rude, like refusing an award. It feels ugly.

Now, all at once, women are refusing to accept sexual aggression as any kind of award, and men are getting fired from their jobs. It feels like an earthquake. Men and women alike find ourselves disoriented, wondering what the rules are. Women know perfectly well that we hate unsolicited sexual attention, but navigate a minefield of male thinking on what "solicit" might mean. We've spent so much life-force on looking good but not too good, being professional but not unapproachable, while the guys just got on with life. And what of the massive costs of permanent vigilance, the tense smiles, declined work assignments and lost chances that are our daily job of trying to avoid assault? Can we get some backpay?

I think we're trying to do that now, as the opening volleys of #MeToo smack us with backlash against backlash. Patriarchy persists because power does not willingly cede its clout; and also, frankly, because women are widely complicit in the assumption that we're separate and not quite equal. If we're woke, we inspect ourselves and others for implicit racial bias, while mostly failing to recognise explicit gender bias, which still runs rampant. Religious faiths that subordinate women flourish on every continent. Nearly every American educational institution pours the lion's share of its athletics budget into the one sport that still excludes women—American football.

Most progressives wouldn't hesitate to attend a football game, or to praise the enlightened new pope—the one who says he's sorry, but women still can't lead his church, or control our reproduction. In heterosexual weddings, religious or secular, the patriarch routinely "gives" his daughter to the groom, after which she's presented to the audience as "Mrs New Patriarch," to joyous applause. We have other options, of course: I kept my name in marriage and gave it to my daughters. But most modern brides still embrace the ritual erasure of their identities, taking the legal name of a new male head of household, as enslaved people used to do when they came to a new plantation owner.

I can already hear the outcry against conflating traditional marriage with slavery. Yes, I know, the marital bargain has changed: women are no longer chattels. Tell me this giving-away and name-changing are just vestiges of a cherished tradition. I'll reply that some of my neighbours here in the south still fly the Confederate flag—not with hate, they insist, but to honour a proud tradition. In either case, a tradition in which people legally control other people doesn't strike me as worth celebrating, even symbolically.

If any contract between men required the non-white one to adopt the legal identity of his Caucasian companion, would we pop the champagne? If any sport wholly excluded people of colour, would it fill stadiums throughout the land? Would we attend a church whose sacred texts consign Latinos to inferior roles? What about galas where black and Asian participants must wear painful shoes and clothes that reveal lots of titillating, well-toned flesh while white people turn up comfortably covered?

No wonder there is confusion about this volcano of outrage against men who objectify and harass. Marriage is not slavery, but a willingness to subvert our very names in our primary partnership might confound everyone's thinking about where women stand in our other relationships with men. And if our sex lives aren't solely ours to control, but also the purview of men of the cloth, why not employers too? We may ache for gender equality but we're rarely framing or fighting for it in the same ways we fight for racial equality. The #MeToo movement can't bring justice to a culture so habituated to misogyny that we can't even fathom parity, and women still dread losing the power we've been taught to use best: our charm.

Years ago, as a college student, I spent a semester abroad in a beautiful, historic city where the two sentences I heard most in English, usually conjoined, were "You want to go for coffee?" and "You want to have sex with me, baby?" I lived near a huge public garden where I wished I could walk or study, but couldn't, without being followed, threatened and subjected to jarring revelations of some creep's penis among the foliages. My experiment in worldliness had me trapped, fuming, in a tiny apartment.

One day in a fit of weird defiance I tied a sofa cushion to my belly under a loose dress and discovered this was the magic charm: I could walk anywhere, unmolested. I carried my after-class false pregnancy to the end of the term, happily ignored by predators. As a lissom 20-year-old I resented my waddly disguise, but came around to a riveting truth: being attractive was less useful to me than being free.

Modern women's magazines promise we don't have to choose, we can be sovereign powers and seductresses both at once. But study the pictures and see an attractiveness imbued with submission and myriad forms of punitive self-alteration. Actually, we have to choose: not one or the other utterly, but some functional point between these poles. It starts with a sober reckoning of how much we really need to be liked by the universe of men. Not all men confuse "liking" with conquest, of course—just the handful of jerks who poison the well, and the larger number who think they are funny. Plus the majority of the US male electorate, who put a boastful assaulter in charge of us all.

This is the point. The universe of men does not merit women's indiscriminate grace. If the #MeToo revolution has proved anything, it's that women live under threat. Not sometimes, but all the time.

We don't have unlimited options about working for male approval, since here in this world that is known as "approval." We also want to be loved, probably we want it too much. But loved. Bear with us while we sort this out, and begin to codify it in the bluntest terms. Enduring some guy's copped feel or a gander at his plumbing is so very much not a Valentine. It is a letter bomb. It can blow up a day, an interview, a job, a home, the very notion of safety inside our bodies.

It shouldn't be this hard to demand safety while we do our work, wear whatever, walk where we need to go. And yet, for countless women enduring harassment on the job, it is this hard, and escape routes are few. The path to freedom is paved with many special words for "hideously demanding person" that only apply to females.

Chaining the links of our experiences behind a hashtag can help supply the courage to be unlovely while we blast an ugly reality into the open. The chain doesn't negate women's individuality or our capacity to trust men individually, nor does it suggest every assault is the same. Raped is not groped is not catcalled on the street: all these are vile and have to stop, but the damages are different. Women who wish to be more than bodies can use our brains to discern context and the need for cultural education. In lieu of beguiling we can be rational, which means giving the accused a fair hearing and a sentence that fits the crime. (Let it also be said, losing executive power is not the death penalty, even if some people are carrying on as if it were.) Polarisation is as obstructive in gender politics as in any other forum. Sympathetic men are valuable allies.

Let's be clear: no woman asks to live in a rape culture: we all want it over, yesterday. Mixed signals about female autonomy won't help bring it down, and neither will asking nicely. Nothing changes until truly powerful offenders start to fall. Feminine instincts for sweetness and apology have no skin in this game. It's really not possible to overreact to uncountable, consecutive days of being humiliated by men who say our experience isn't real, or that we like it actually, or are cute when we're mad. Anger has to go somewhere—if not out then inward, in a psychic thermodynamics that can turn a nation of women into pressure cookers. Watching the election of a predator-in-chief seems to have popped the lid off the can. We've found a voice, and now is a good time to use it, in a tone that will not be mistaken for flirtation.

Don't say that to me. Don't do that to me. I hate it.

"*It is also about having conversations with our friends, families and communities about where sexist behaviors and attitudes come from and how we should go about fixing them.*"

# To Stop Sexual Harassment, We Need to Change Society

*Elena Gagovska*

*In the following viewpoint, Elena Gagovska relates times she was the victim of sexual harassment in school. She notes that sharing anecdotes like this lets people know how common sexual harassment is. Many men seem to think only a few terrible, powerful celebrities commit offenses. In reality, these are an everyday occurrence for most women, and they make women feel unsafe. The author says we must challenge sexism and misogyny, the ingrained prejudice against women. We must recognize that our friends and families can be guilty of sexual violence. Elena Gagovska is from Macedonia. She wrote this as a student in the Humanities, Arts, and Social Thought program at Bard College Berlin in Germany.*

"#MeToo: A Conversation We Must Not Stop Having," by Elena Gagovska, Bard College Berlin, January 14, 2018. Reprinted by permission.

As you read, consider the following questions:

1. What is the value in sharing anecdotes about harassment, according to this author?
2. Why is it important to recognize that ordinary people we know may be guilty of sexual harassment or assault?
3. How does society allow sexual harassment and assault to continue?

The first time someone touched me without my consent, I was in middle school. I think it was in the 7th grade and I was turned to my friends who were sitting at the desk behind me, when a boy grabbed my left breast out of nowhere. I was wearing a purple sweater and a training bra that barely gave any shape to my still-growing breasts. At least, I think that was the first time. It happened a lot in my middle school; it definitely happened to most of my friends.

I tried to speak out. I told our homeroom teacher and she yelled at the boys in our class in front of the girls, telling them that this was wrong. But no real disciplinary measures were taken. Most of the boys (at least in my class) engaged in non-consensual touching, and it seemed that the school didn't want to deal with disciplining such a large number of students. Eventually, our complaints were simply met with different versions of "boys will be boys". They were just in "that phase" when they were discovering their sexual urges and, apparently, no one was going to stop these boys from acting on them.

Two memories from middle school stand out. The first is of a few of the more "popular" boys making fun of another, less "popular," boy—we'll call him Filip—because he had never felt a girl's butt. I even remember thinking it strange that he hadn't. I, a girl, had internalized the gendered logic that the boys in my class had absorbed and then recreated. What made one masculine was sexual power over feminine people. Eventually, Filip got this mark of masculinity, too. There was no adult around to tell them that this logic was harmful because, of course, this was the logic of the adult world as well.

The other memory is of me standing in the back of the classroom where we had Macedonian language and literature classes, negotiating my sexual safety with one of the aforementioned "popular" boys:

> "If you let me grab your ass, I'll leave you alone," he assured me.
> "Fine," I reluctantly agreed. He grabbed one of my butt cheeks. But it was not the last time. I wasn't too shocked when he broke his promise.

I have had many more experiences like these after middle school because these boys, and the boys that came before them, had grown up into young adults. Some became teenagers who cat-called. Others became young men with girlfriends they didn't see as equals. They became uncles who said inappropriate things at the dinner table. Many of those who found themselves on top of professional hierarchies became men who were able to abuse their positions of power. And then, some became sexual predators and rapists. Some of these people are men we do not know, but some we know very well. And that makes telling these stories all the more difficult.

I didn't write #MeToo when the campaign took off because I didn't want to scare my parents with the reality of their daughter having experienced sexual harassment. I should have written it. I definitely should have. I think a part of me didn't write it because it's not fun to talk about the times when I've felt violated. But it is important to talk about them. So, yes, sadly, me too. And here are some of the times it's happened:

I was cat-called three times when walking to meet a friend for coffee in Skopje. It was 3pm in July, and I was wearing a dress.

I was walking home one winter break when a middle-aged man fixing his car in the middle of the night for some reason said "come on in, sweetie." It was 2:30am, I was wearing my warm grey skirt, I was 16, and I was alone.

I was at a doctor's appointment when one of my doctors said to the other, "doesn't she catch your eye?" That was one of the least offensive things he said or did during our interactions—he ended up poking my butt at a later appointment. I was wearing jeans and a top. It was 1pm in a hospital.

I was at a party when an acquaintance asked if he could grab my butt so that he could rate it. I said no, but he did it anyway. He gave me an eight. He asked me to rate his butt afterwards and I touched it because I think I wanted to feel like his touching was not un-consensual when it definitely was. "I have a girlfriend, but the question is how quiet you can keep," he said, placing himself uncomfortably close to me later at the party after I had told him that I was not interested multiple times. Eventually, he gave up. I was a junior in high school. It was July, and I was wearing a blue skirt.

I was at Alexanderplatz when a teenage boy—probably sixteen or seventeen—ran towards me and grabbed my breast. The boy's friends pulled him away and then one of them tried to high five me as a reward for saving me from his horrible friend. I high-fived him back because I wanted them to leave. I was with two friends who were as stunned as I was. One of them froze, the other started yelling at them—both legitimate responses. It was 4am in August and I was wearing shorts.

I was in Friedrichshain when a man tried to follow me on an empty street. I had a panic attack in the tram and I texted a friend who suggested that I get pepper spray. I began to calm down by the time I got to S+U Pankow, but then another man asked me for directions. I told him where to go but instead he started following me and told me that I had beautiful eyes. He asked me if he could walk with me and I said that I just wanted to go home. He then straight up asked me if I was scared of him and I repeated that I wanted to go home. He left me alone, but I could not stop having panic attacks for most of the night. It was two months ago at 2am, and I was wearing jeans and heeled boots.

I haven't had the worst experiences. Not by a long shot. But this isn't a competition. This article isn't just about the specifics of my experiences. It's about the similarities between my experiences and the experiences of other women.[1] Because, no, this is not just about a collection of anecdotes, this is about recognition and dismantlement of a system that produces these anecdotes.

That said, it is not surprising that the #MeToo movement started picking up steam through anecdotes. When we give an indistinguishable monster a human face, the issue becomes more concrete. However, the problem with associating specific individuals with a certain societal problem is that people are liable to view that problem as being person-specific. The face of sexual harassment now is no longer a nondescript male face; it is Harvey Weinstein's face. I've heard men around me talk about Weinstein being a pervert. They aren't wrong. But they talk about Weinstein as if he is the only man who has acted like this. They talk about him like their friends, brothers and fathers could not possibly be capable of similar behavior. They talk about him like the women they know have never had a Harvey in their lives. Sexual harassment and assault are being abstracted to the idea of powerful men who can hide behind assistants, lawyers and other powerful friends that we don't think to look into our own backyards.

To battle the prevailing sexism, it is not enough to see rich actresses wearing black designer dresses at the Golden Globes speak about these issues or their powerful male counterparts get taken down. Yes, we definitely should see men like Weinstein and Trump reprimanded. However, if we focus our punishment on them alone without thinking about the systemic changes that need to happen in order to reduce (and hopefully eradicate) sexual harassment, the battle will not be won. But it is not only about disciplinary/punitive measures for sexual harassers. It is also about having conversations with our friends, families and communities about where sexist behaviors and attitudes come from and how we should go about fixing them. I would like to quote Jessica Delgato's Public Seminar article:

> This is a time of soul searching for men. It is a time of risk and bravery for both women and men. It is not fun for anyone. It

is painful and scary and traumatizing and re-traumatizing. It is disruptive and destructive. Friends will be lost. Families will be torn up. Communities will be fractured.[2]

Delgato writes of the difficult but necessary conversations ahead. Despite what some people will have you believe, the hegemony is not feminist. Our societies have been built on gender roles, sexism and misogyny. We have had to fight for things from the right to work to the right to vote to the right to an abortion. Some of these fights are still ongoing. But our fights are not ones that strive solely for legal victories. For true female and human liberation, we must work on deconstructing the patriarchal structures that affect us all. Though gender is a complex concept that merits more than just an article-length explanation, a lot of us already understand that it is something that is socially constructed. Some behaviors, such as aggression, are encouraged for men but discouraged for women.

Gender and gender roles are so pervasive that they affect the clothes we wear, the toys children play with, who pays on first dates, who gets to be in charge in both the private and public sphere. It is these gender roles, among many other things, that create the patriarchal value system we live under—the same system that teaches men to act in certain ways around women. When our lives are so shaped by the gendered roles we play every day, it is immensely difficult to break out of them, let alone dismantle the system that helps maintain them.

However, this dismantlement will not begin to happen if we abstract the concept of patriarchy or the consequent sexual harassment to Hollywood. We must recognize that patriarchy and misogyny are systems that haunt every aspect of our lives. Yes, they affect and are perpetuated by our friends, family and loved ones as well as the Weinsteins of the world. This does not make these people necessarily bad or irredeemable. It just means that there is a lot of work to be done by everyone.

When talking about sexual violence, people like to point out that sometimes these gender roles are reversed and that women can also be perpetrators. Certainly there are exceptions, and certainly men can also be victims of sexual violence (usually perpetrated by other men).[3] This isn't to say that male victims of sexual abuse shouldn't use the hashtag, but it seems to me that #MeToo is primarily about acknowledging that the structures that allow for sexual violence against women by men to be depressingly common. It is about understanding that in sexual assault cases the majority of the perpetrators are men and the majority of the victims are women—not only because on average women are physically weaker than men, but also because we have a culture that encourages male sexual dominance and aggression and simultaneously does not believe that women could be subjected to and victims of it.

Still, not everyone affected most negatively by patriarchy will be able to speak about their experiences. No matter how limited, I still have a platform to write about my experiences. Sadly, #MeToo didn't catch the world's attention until famous actresses started sharing their stories. Not everyone is aware of the fact that a black woman named Tarana Burke started the original #MeToo campaign in 2007. The most silenced victims of sexual violence are those who lack social and economic power i.e. marginalized people such as women of color, working class women, people with disabilities, queer and trans people. During a Democracy Now! interview, Burke said:

> For every R. Kelly or Bill Cosby or Harvey Weinstein, there's, you know, the owner of the grocery store, the coach, the teacher, the neighbor, who are doing the same things. But we don't pay attention until it's a big name. And we don't pay attention 'til it's a big celebrity. But this work is ongoing, because this is pervasive.[4]

In a sense, Tarana Burke expresses the pervasive nature of the patriarchal values that encourage sexually abusive behavior. It is not simply a Hollywood problem; it is a societal problem. It is still good to make examples out of powerful men, but punishing them without addressing our culture of misogyny, which frequently refuses to believe victims of sexual harassment and assault, will not ensure the necessary progress that will benefit the majority of people. The four point anti-harassment action plan set forth by influential Hollywood actresses such as Eva Longoria includes a point about "a legal defense fund, backed by $13 million in donations, to help less privileged women"[5] which acknowledges the class dimension of this issue. Indeed, this is a very good start, but our conversation must be bigger than that.

I would like to return to the boys and girls at the beginning of this article because that is where this story truly begins and recreates itself generation after generation. It will certainly not be easy to raise children in a way that is free from patriarchy and misogyny after the parents themselves have been raised and lived within the frameworks of these systems, but it is definitely possible to raise future generations to be at the very least less sexist than the ones that came before them. That being said, I do have hope. Change is constantly happening, and change for the better is not impossible. My little cousin complained to me about some boys yelling at her from a distance and she labeled it catcalling. She and others from her generation already possess some of the vocabulary to name these problematic behaviors whereas I hadn't even heard of feminism until 9th or 10th grade in high school. This isn't to say that our work is done, but the discourse is changing, and that is a good thing. Perhaps our parenting styles and societal values will follow along sooner rather than later.

But this process will not be quick; it is far from easy to address these deep-seated issues. It is not enjoyable to have arguments about gender with your family members or to have male acquaintances use the word "Feminazi," or to write about occasions when men have made you and still make you feel unsafe. To quote Delgato: "We speak even though we don't want to." She's right.[6] I know that at least I don't want to. Writing this whole article has been incredibly uncomfortable, but here I am. Here we are.

## Notes

1. Men may also be victims of sexual harassment and assault, but in this article I will be focusing on people who present and are perceived as women.

2. Delgato, Jessica. *The Reckoning*. Public Seminar. December 26, 2017.
3. More in this link: http://www.michigan.gov/documents/datingviolence/DHS-DatingViolence-MaleSurvivors_198439_7.pdf
4. Meet Tarana Burke, Activist Who Started "Me Too" Campaign to Ignite Conversation on Sexual Assault. Democracy Now! October 17, 2017.
5. Buckley, Cara. Powerful Hollywood Women Unveil Anti-Harassment Action Plan. The New York Times. January 1, 2018.
6. Ibid. Delgato.

# Periodical and Internet Sources Bibliography

*The following articles have been selected to supplement the diverse views presented in this chapter.*

Candace Bertotti and David Maxfield, "Most People Are Supportive of #MeToo. But Will Workplaces Actually Change?" Harvard Business Review, July 10, 2018. https://hbr.org/2018/07/most-people-are-supportive-of-metoo-but-will-workplaces-actually-change.

Daniela Ceron, "How Women of Color Are Discussed in Hashtag Feminist Movements," *Elon Journal of Undergraduate Research in Communications*, Vol. 9, No. 2, Fall 2018. https://www.elon.edu/u/academics/communications/journal/wp.../07-Ceron.pdf.

Noreen Farrell, "Our Bodies on the Line: Latina Equal Pay and #MeToo," Equal Rights Advocates, Nov 1, 2018. https://www.equalrights.org/our-bodies-on-the-line-latina-equal-pay-and-metoo/.

Johanna Ferreira, "How the #MeToo Movement Impacts Latinas," Hip Latina, January 25, 2018. https://hiplatina.com/metoo-movement-impacts-latinas/.

Elena Gagovska, "#MeToo: A Conversation We Must Not Stop Having," Die Bärliner Blog, https://theleftberlin.wordpress.com/current-debates/metoo-a-conversation-we-must-not-stop-having/.

Miriam Haughton, "Gender, Power and Tipping Points," RTÉ, March 8, 2018. https://www.rte.ie/eile/brainstorm/2018/0306/945400-gender-power-and-tipping-points/.

Grace Huang, "How to Make Sure Immigrant Women Aren't Left out of Me Too," Asian Pacific Institute on Gender Based Violence, June 2018. https://www.api-gbv.org/resources/make-sure-immigrant-women-arent-left/.

Charisse Jones, "When Will MeToo Become WeToo? Some Say Voices of Black Women, Working Class Left Out," *USA Today*, October 5, 2018. https://www.usatoday.com/story/money/2018/10/05/metoo-movement-lacks-diversity-blacks-working-class-sexual-harassment/1443105002/.

Beh Lih Yieh, "In Asia, Saying #MeToo Still Dangerous for Some Women," Thompson Reuters Foundation News, December 17, 2018. http://news.trust.org//item/20181217150559-ib3wa/

Leah Litman, "#MeToo Series: When Will #MeToo Become #WeToo?" Take Care, April 9, 2018. https://takecareblog.com/blog/metoo-series-when-will-metoo-become-wetoo.

Arwa Mahdawi, "The Future of #MeToo: 'The Movement Is Bigger than Asia Argento,'" *Guardian*, September 2, 2018. https://www.theguardian.com/world/2018/sep/01/metoo-movement-asia-argento-rose-mcgowan.

Lucy Marcus, "Why #MeToo Is the Beginning of a Culture of Accountability," We Form, February 22, 2018. https://www.weforum.org/agenda/2018/02/the-sexual-harassment-reckoning.

Christina Pazzanese and Colleen Walsh, "#MeToo Surge Could Change Society in Pivotal Ways," *Harvard Gazette*, December 21, 2017. https://news.harvard.edu/gazette/story/2017/12/metoo-surge-could-change-society-in-pivotal-ways-harvard-analysts-say/.

Jessica Prois and Carolina Moreno, "The #MeToo Movement Looks Different for Women of Color. Here Are 10 Stories," Huffington Post, January 2, 2018. https://www.huffingtonpost.com/entry/women-of-color-me-too_us_5a442d73e4b0b0e5a7a4992c.

Jeffrey Tobias, "Women at the Tipping Point: The Effect of the #MeToo Momentum," Huffington Post, December 14, 2017. https://www.huffingtonpost.com/entry/women-at-the-tipping-point-the-effect-of-the-metoo_us_5a32eb30e4b0e7f1200cf96a.

# For Further Discussion

## Chapter 1

1. Viewpoints 2 and 4 suggest that MeToo is clarifying guidelines around sex and consent. This should help men avoid behavior that could get them in trouble. Do you see the movement as making guidelines clearer or more confusing? How so?

2. Viewpoint 3 says that MeToo has encouraged discussions about sexual harassment and assault. This has allowed male victims to speak up, which helps men. When issues are publicly discussed, does that make it easier for people to share their stories? What other ways might the movement help men?

3. Viewpoint 5 says MeToo treats women like children who need protection. The author feels that the movement is doing damage. Viewpoint 6 shares some of the specific outcomes of the movement. Has MeToo done more harm, or more good? What evidence supports your view?

## Chapter 2

1. Viewpoint 1 says people should be tried in court, with a presumption of innocence. Should we always assume people are innocent until proven guilty? How does that fit with our world of instantly sharing claims by social media?

2. Viewpoint 2 says the MeToo movement should not only be about legal claims. It should address rape culture and the imbalance of power in society. Are these social problems that cannot be handled by the law? How can we tackle them? Do news articles and discussions help? Why or why not?

3.  Women and girls have always suffered from sexual harassment and violence. The law often does not protect them. Now many men are afraid they may be falsely accused of sexual harassment or assault. What can we do to ensure women are protected? If a few men are falsely accused, and in exchange many women are protected from future harassment, is that a reasonable trade? Why or why not?

## Chapter 3

1.  Should we immediately believe people who claim they have been harassed? Should we demand absolute proof? How can we balance believing victims with demanding evidence?

2.  Viewpoint 4 discusses "Trial by Twitter." Many victims of harassment and assault can't prove their claims. Social media gives them a way to find some justice. Is it fair to accuse people on social media, if you're not willing to take them to court? Why or why not? What are the advantages and disadvantages to shaming someone versus getting the law involved?

3.  Viewpoint 6 discusses MeToo accusations against women. The author notes that people can be both victims and offenders when it comes to harassment. She argues that harassment is a matter of power, not sex. How does power play into harassment? What can we do about it? Should everyone be held to the same standard, regardless of their sex, gender identity, or sexual orientation? Why or why not?

## Chapter 4

1. Viewpoint 3 claims the MeToo movement does not fully understand and support black women. What role does race play in harassment and assault? How can people of different races support each other? How might we change society and the government to equally protect everyone?

2. Have you witnessed instances when men made women feel uncomfortable? Do you think other people understand how common harassment is? Should we take every incident seriously, or should we focus on physical assault and shrug off minor encounters? What counts as minor? Who gets to decide?

3. How does talking about our experiences help us or others? Are there disadvantages? What should people do when they hear a friend or family member behaving badly?

# Organizations to Contact

*The editors have compiled the following list of organizations concerned with the issues debated in this book. The descriptions are derived from materials provided by the organizations. All have publications or information available for interested readers. The list was compiled on the date of publication of the present volume; the information provided here may change. Be aware that many organizations take several weeks or longer to respond to inquiries, so allow as much time as possible.*

### Asian Pacific Institute on Gender Based Violence

500 12th Street, Suite 330
Oakland, CA 94607
(415) 568-3315
email: info@api-gbv.org
website: www.api-gbv.org

This site links to articles, statistics, and resources for gender-based violence. It focuses on immigrant and refugee women as well as those living in Asia and the Pacific Islands.

### Equality Now

125 Maiden Lane, 9th Floor, Suite B
New York NY 10038
(212) 586-0906
email: info@equalitynow.org
website: www.equalitynow.org

Equality Now wants to eliminate violence and discrimination against women and girls around the world through legal action. The website has publications and fact sheets.

**Equal Rights Advocates**

1170 Market Street, Suite 700
San Francisco, CA 94102
(415) 621-0672
email: info@equalrights.org
website: www.equalrights.org

Equal Rights Advocates protects and expands economic and educational access and opportunities for women and girls.

**Girls for Gender Equity (GGE)**

25 Chapel St.
Brooklyn, NY 11201
(718) 857-1393
email: press@metoomvmt.org.
website: www.ggenyc.org

GGE works to end gender-based violence. It addresses racism, sexism, transphobia, homophobia, and economic inequality. GGE leads healing circles for youth and combats sexual harassment in schools.

**MaleSurvivor**

PO Box 276
Long Valley, NJ 07853
email form: www.malesurvivor.org/contact-us
website: www.malesurvivor.org/index.php

MaleSurvivor offers support and resources to male sexual assault survivors, their families, and their allies. Resources for survivors include support groups, discussion forums, and articles.

**MeToo**

email: info@metoomvmt.org
website: metoomvmt.org

The "me too" movement was founded in 2006 to help survivors of sexual violence, particularly young women of color. It connects survivors and their allies with resources, gathers sexual violence research, and supports political change.

### The National Center for Transgender Equality (NCTE)

1133 19th Street NW, Suite 302
Washington, DC 20036
(202) 642-4542
email: ncte@transequality.org
website: transequality.org

NCTE supports transgender equality. Its website features a Know Your Rights section that covers discrimination and sexual harassment.

### National Organization for Men Against Sexism (NOMAS)

3500 E. 17th Avenue
Denver, CO 80206
(303) 997-9581
email: info@nomas.org
website: http://nomas.org

NOMAS is an activist organization supporting positive changes for men. The website provides resources, a reading list, and a blog. Task groups tackle ending violence, eliminating racism, and much more.

### National Organization for Women (NOW)

1100 H Street NW, Suite 300
Washington, DC 20005
(202) 628-8669
email: https://now.org/about/contact-us
website: now.org

NOW is a grassroots group dedicated to women's rights, with hundreds of chapters around the country. It promotes the equal rights of all women and girls in all aspects of life. Get news and learn how you can get involved.

**National Resource Center on Domestic Violence**

6041 Linglestown Road
Harrisburg, PA 17112
(800) 537-2238
website: vawnet.org
contact form: https://vawnet.org/contact

The site hosts a resource library with material on violence against women and related issues. It pays particular attention to how violence intersects with forms of oppression.

**National Sexual Violence Resource Center (NSVRC)**

2101 N Front Street
Governor's Plaza North, Building #2
Harrisburg, PA 17110
(717) 909-0710
website: www.nsvrc.org
contact form: https://www.nsvrc.org/contact

NSVRC offers information relating to sexual violence, including a large legal resource library.

**ProMundo**

1367 Connecticut Avenue NW
Washington, DC 20036
(202) 588-0060
email: contact@promundoglobal.org
website: promundoglobal.org

Promundo works to promote gender justice and prevent violence. It engages men and boys in partnership with women and girls. Learn about their work and find news and resources.

**Rape, Abuse & Incest National Network (RAINN)**

1220 L Street NW, Suite 505
Washington, DC 20005
(800) 656-4673
website: www.rainn.org
contact form: https://www.rainn.org/submit-question

RAINN is the largest anti-sexual violence organization in the United States. RAINN created and operates the National Sexual Assault Hotline. It carries out programs to prevent sexual violence, help survivors, and ensure that perpetrators are brought to justice.

**Rice University Center for the Study of Women, Gender, and Sexuality**

6100 Main Street
Houston, TX 77005-1892
(713) 348-0000
email: cswgs@rice.edu
website: https://cswgs.rice.edu

The center fosters research and teaching on topics relating to women, gender, and sexuality. Read articles in the Feminist Forum.

**University of Warwick Center for the Study of Women and Gender (CSWG)**

Social Sciences Building, the University of Warwick
Coventry, CV4 7AL
United Kingdom
email directory: https://warwick.ac.uk/fac/soc/sociology/staff/
website: https://warwick.ac.uk/fac/soc/sociology/research/centres/gender/

CSWG is a British social sciences center. It supports research and teaching in women's, gender, and feminist studies.

## White Ribbon

36 Eglinton Avenue W, Suite 603
Toronto, ON M4R 1A1
Canada
(416) 920-6684
email: info@whiteribbon.ca
website: www.whiteribbon.ca

White Ribbon is a movement of men and boys. It works to end violence against women and girls, and to promote gender equity, healthy relationships, and a new vision of masculinity. Take their pledge, learn about their projects, and find out what you can do.

# Bibliography of Books

Chimamanda Ngozi Adichie. *We Should All Be Feminists*. New York, NY: Anchor Books, 2015.

Karen Catlin. *Better Allies: Everyday Actions to Create Inclusive, Engaging Workplaces*. Better Allies Press, 2019.

Emily Chang. *Brotopia*. New York, NY: Penguin, 2018.

Jennifer K. Crittenden. *What's a Guy to Do?: How to Work with Women*. San Diego, CA: Whistling Rabbit Press, 2018.

Shannon N. Davis. *Gender in the Twenty-First Century: The Stalled Revolution and the Road to Equality*. Berkeley, CA: University of California Press, 2017.

Carrie Fisher. *The Princess Diarist*. New York, NY: E. P. Dutton, 2016.

Leymah Gbowee. *Mighty Be Our Powers: How Sisterhood, Prayer, and Sex Changed a Nation at War*. New York, NY: Beast Books, 2013.

Linda Gordan Howard. *The Sexual Harassment Handbook: Everything You Need to Know Before Someone Calls a Lawyer*. Newburyport, MA: Weiser, 2007.

Kelly Jensen. *Here We Are: Feminism for the Real World*. Chapel Hill, NC: Algonquin Young Readers, 2017.

Sam Killermann. *A Guide to Gender: The Social Justice Advocate's Handbook*. Second edition. Austin, TX: Impetus Books, 2017

Andrea S. Kramer. *Breaking Through Bias: Communication Techniques for Women to Succeed at Work*. Abingdon, England: Routledge, 2016.

Joanne Lipman. *That's What She Said: What Men Need to Know (and Women Need to Tell Them) About Working Together*. New York, NY: William Morrow, 2018.

Kate Manne. *Down Girl: The Logic of Misogyny.* Oxford, England: Oxford University Press, 2019.

Jack Myers. *The Future of Men: Men on Trial.* Oakland, CA: Inkshares, 2016.

Anne Helen Petersen. *Too Fat, Too Slutty, Too Loud: The Rise and Reign of the Unruly Woman.* New York, NY: Plume, 2017.

Joni Seager. *The Women's Atlas.* New York, NY: Penguin Books, 2018.

Rebecca Solnit. *Men Explain Things to Me.* London, England: Granta, 2001.

# Index